SECOND CHANCE

by
William H. Pew

Dedication

This book is dedicated to our Creator and Savior, the Lord Jesus Christ, who alone is worthy to receive all glory and power.

I thank those who performed CPR on me and who God used as His servants and gave the necessary strength to continue CPR until the ambulance arrived, even though they were convinced I was dead.

I thank Bill Bright of Campus Crusade who, many years ago, showed me the foundation for Christian living through The Four Spiritual Laws and basic Bible studies.

I thank God daily for my wife and family, for the support they gave me through my experience, and for the peace I have in knowing that we will someday be in heaven as a family.

I thank God for the people, ministries, books, films, and knowledge that have helped me to grow spiritually. I thank God for Jack Van Impe, Moody Bible Institute, Lehman Strauss, James Kennedy, Chuck Colson, Joe Stowell, and many others.

Contents

FOREWORD

William Pew, a man of multiplied attributes, has been chosen, blessed, and revived from the "jaws of death" for a purpose—the revitalization of stagnant Christianity.

In writing a foreword for this book, which has stirred every fiber of my being, I wondered how I could best describe Bill. I decided to use alliteration. In total honesty, terms like character, chivalry, conscientiousness, consecration, contagion, and contemplation are certainly not exaggerations but veritable expressions of this dedicated servant of God.

When I first met Bill, who was to become my close friend, I immediately concluded that soul-winning and witnessing were the primary goals of his existence. Although he had built one of the most successful manufacturing companies of our day, this business enterprise took second place in his life. Jesus Christ was Lord of all—including his possessions.

When Bill had his encounter with cardiac arrest and was brought back from the jaws of death, God, in His providence, allowed Rexella and me to be in the very area ministering. The first thing Bill said to us after being give his "Second Chance" was: "I want to do more for the Lord!"

Rexella and I wondered how this totally dedicated man could possibly do more than what he had always done—which was to constantly tell others about the Way, the Truth, and the Life.

Today William Pew's only reason for existing is to win as many as he can before Christ calls him home. It's also his motive for writing this thrilling, informative book.

Bill is an industrialist, not a journalist. What you are about to read is from the burning heart of a layman. However, as I read chapter after chapter, my heart was also aflame because I felt the imprint of the Holy Spirit upon the pages of *Second Chance*.

To sum up my alliterative assessment of Bill Pew, I believe I can best describe the author of this book as being a man of courage, conviction, and compassion. You will experience all these qualities as you read the story of a man who literally died and lived again.

Jack Van Impe
Troy, Michigan, 1991

Chapter 1

Sudden Cardiac Death

It was one of those lazy February afternoons in Florida. I was puttering around home with nothing in particular to do and my wife was at her ceramics class. It was a great day to go try the golf pointers the club pro had given me the week before. Within minutes I was at the driving range, addressing the ball for my first swing of the day.

Then I dropped dead!

It came without warning. I wasn't short of breath. No pains. I had been feeling fine. In fact, I had been to the doctor for a physical every year and I felt great. I fully expected to live another 35 years to be 100. But suddenly it looked like I was on my way to joining the 1,500 Americans who die every day of cardiac arrest.

My sudden death was witnessed by three (very startled!) strangers who were nearby. All three, it turned out, knew cardiac pulmonary resuscitation (CPR). They immediately sized up the situation, fully aware that it only takes minutes without blood circulation for the brain to suffer permanent damage. Without wasting a second, they began pumping my chest to keep the blood flowing and giving me mouth-to-mouth resuscitation to keep air in my lungs.

Though the paramedics had been called almost as soon as I hit the ground, there was no sign of them after 10 minutes. My would-be rescuers knew that, even with expert CPR, my chances of living after that long were under 10 percent and fading. Actually, only 5 percent of those suffering cardiac arrest outside a hospital survive, primarily because of the time it takes the emergency medical service to arrive.

The three gave up hope. Twenty minutes passed, and they still worked on, even though they couldn't rouse a heartbeat or a breath. Thirty minutes. Finally, the paramedics arrived after negotiating a traffic snarl that had stretched a short drive into a full half-hour one. Taking over for my by-now exhausted rescuers, they administered a shot, oxygen, and electrical defibrillations.

Five powerful electrical impulses jolted my body. No response. It looked like I'd retired my golf clubs for good. In fact, as I was lifted into the ambulance a bystander commented, "Well, if you've got to go, there's no better way for a golfer to die than while he's playing golf!"

One in a million

On the way to the hospital, one of the paramedics decided to give me one more charge. Only God knows why, but it was the try that jump-started my heart!

After two days in intensive care in Naples, Florida, I was helicoptered to the cardiac unit at Ft. Meyers Medical Center for further treatment. When I finally became aware of my surroundings again—about five days after teeing up—they were shaving my body in preparation for triple bypass surgery.

I awoke from surgery with a little numbness in my chest. My left leg hurt where a vein had been removed for my surgery. But otherwise I had no pain. I soon learned that I had just become a living statistic. I am the ONE in "one in a million," the one lone survivor despite incredible odds. It would have been much more reasonable to assume, as my fellow golfers had, that I would be among the 999,999 who don't make it. But not this time.

You can believe me when I say that you never know how dear life is until you have an experience like the one I had. In fact, in a way, I wish all this could have happened years ago. Why? Because now I realize more than ever that God has a special purpose for my life. My second opportunity to live allows me to accomplish it.

Interestingly enough, the woman (Julie Sprague) and two men (Joe Cannavo and his son-in-law, Nick Venn) who worked so feverishly to save my life all have a strong faith in God. In fact, Joe told me later that every time he applied the rhythmic CPR pumping action to my chest, he prayed in short bursts of expelled breath, "Lord, don't let him die! Lord, don't let him die!" We've all become friends since that day, and not one of us feels we were at the driving range that afternoon at the same time by chance.

When I eventually returned home from the hospital, reporters were on hand to follow up the original report of my death. Did I have an out-of-body experience, looking on as a crowd gathered around the three strangers working persistently to save me? Had I gone through a tunnel? Did I see bright lights during that long half-hour?

Actually, none of the above was true. I don't remember a thing! Not the frantic efforts to revive me. Not the electric charges. Not even the bypass surgery later. Even the extensive conversations that my family tells me I had with them and others during those days are nowhere to be found in my mind! I remember absolutely nothing.

I don't have a clue as to why I have no memory of those days. But I'm sure I know why I've been allowed to live again. That's what counts. I'm absolutely certain God wants me to share with others what it means to know Him personally.

Making up for lost time

Don't get me wrong. This isn't the story of someone who lived a miserable life and wants to make things right this time around. Not at all. Ever since the age of nine, I've been part of God's family. And I had two great parents who raised me in a godly home. The truth is, I've always enjoyed life.

But now I realize more than ever how much I have to live for. The days are brighter, my home feels like a palace to me, I'm married to the prettiest girl I've ever seen, and my friends and neighbors are wonderful. If you think that sounds like a man who has come to see life with a new appreciation, you're exactly right!

If you'd had a close brush with death and were given a second chance, don't you think you'd do things differently? I think you would, just like I did. After all, death is man's greatest enemy, man's greatest fear. To feel its icy grasp and then to be given my life back again—well, I just wanted to make sure my life counted for God from that moment on.

I wish I could tell you that you, too, will have a second chance to live...but I can't. I escaped death's grasp once, but I know that eventually death will return. And someday death will come for you, too. But as long as you can read this, there's still time for you to make sure you're prepared for that moment.

You must be born again

When my time comes (again!), I can face death peacefully. I was ready to go the first time, though I had no idea it would be so sudden. And I'll be prepared the next time, whenever "next time" arrives. But I want YOU to be ready. You can be. You only need one thing in your life—Jesus Christ.

Jesus can make a difference in your life. He did for me. Give Him your life and I guarantee He will do for you what He promised in John 10:10—*I have come that* [you] *may have life, and have it to the full.*

Abundant life can be yours—now and when you die. Whenever people hear the good news of Jesus Christ and respond in faith to Him, He gives them new, abundant, eternal life. He is the only answer for your life. He is the only solution for this country and the world.

Even as I laid there, dying, my body medically dead, I knew my spirit was alive in the power of Jesus Christ because I had been born again by His blood. I have the gift of abundant life—and it can be yours!

You can't buy this abundant life. There's nothing you can do to earn it. The Bible says, *For it is by grace you have been saved, through faith—and this not from yourselves, it is the gift of God—not by works, so that no one can boast* (Ephesians 2:8,9). All you have to do is believe and receive.

Jesus said, *Here I am! I stand at the door and knock. If anyone hears my voice and opens the door, I will come in and eat with him, and he with me* (Revelation 3:20). When you answer, "I do!" then you are born again and become a child of God.

In John 3, Nicodemus, a well-known religious leader, came to Jesus and asked how he could enter the kingdom of God. Nicodemus was a Pharisee. He tried to live by the Ten Commandments and all the laws of his religion. Yet, Jesus told him, *Unless a man is born again, he cannot see the kingdom of God* (John 3:3). The words *born again* sound too religious for many people, but the truth remains—to have eternal life in God's kingdom, you MUST be born again.

What kind of person are you?

I believe there are three types of people in the world:

1. The Natural Person
2. The Carnal Person
3. The Spiritual Person

The **Natural Person** is one who has never accepted Christ. His sins are unforgiven, and when he dies, the Bible says he will be separated from God for eternity.

The **Carnal Person** is one who has accepted Christ but is still a spiritual baby. He hasn't grown spiritually.

Chuck Colson tells the story about Mickey Cohen, a well-known gangster in New York City. Mickey was into money rackets, murder, prostitution, etc.

One day as Mickey was riding through the streets of the city, he saw a line of cars turning into a parking lot and a crowd of people going into a large building. He asked his chauffeur, "What's going on there?" His chauffeur told him that Billy Graham was having a crusade meeting there. Mickey was curious. He told his chauffeur to pull over and he went inside.

Billy's message sounded good to Mickey. He

liked the idea that after this life he could go to a place where there was no suffering or pain and everything would be just right. At the close of the service, he went down front and went through the prayer of salvation.

Several weeks passed, but there was no change in the way Mickey Cohen lived. Finally, a group of Christian men went to see him. They told Mickey he couldn't do the things he was doing as a Christian.

Mickey replied, "Why not? There are Christian lawyers, Christian doctors, and Christian businessmen. Why not a Christian gangster?"

They told Mickey, "Now that you are a Christian, you are a changed man. You must get rid of the old things and sin in your life and start living for the Lord. Second Corinthians 5:17 says, *If anyone is in Christ, he is a new creation; the old has gone, the new has come!* You must grow as a Christian. Simply being hatched is not enough—you need to fly."

Mickey said, "If that is Christianity, I don't want any part of it!"

A short time later, Mickey's body was found in a motel room, riddled with bullets. He had a choice, but he had refused it because he didn't want to change and become the person God wanted him to be.

There are too many Christians who haven't given up their old lifestyles. They have accepted Christ, but there are no big changes in their lives. They are carnal people.

The **Spiritual Person** is one who has accepted Jesus Christ and who continues to grow spiritually. He practices what I like to call "spiritual breathing." Every day he breathes in spiritual things from the Word of God (the Bible) and exhales unspiritual things from his life. He gets rid of the sin in his life through prayer and Bible study.

If you are still a Natural Person and have not accepted Jesus Christ as Lord and Savior, I urge you to do so now.

REALIZE that Jesus is the Son of God who died for you on the cross.

REPENT by asking God to forgive you of your sin.

RECEIVE Jesus Christ by faith as Savior and Lord of your life. For, *to all who received him, to those who believed in his name* [Jesus], *he gave the right to become children of God* (John 1:12).

RESPOND to Jesus in obedience. For Jesus said, *If anyone would come after me, he must deny himself and take up his cross daily and follow me* (Luke 9:23).

On that fateful day in February 1988 when I died, I had perfect peace. As a child of God, you, too, no longer have to fear death. The grave may hold your body, but you will live on forever with Jesus Christ in heaven. First John 5:11-13 says, *This is the testimony: God has given us eternal life, and this life is in his Son. He who has the Son has life; he who does not have the Son of God does not have life. I write these things to you who believe in the name of the Son of God so that you may know that you have eternal life.*

This is the "Blessed Assurance" we sing about— we have eternal life through Jesus Christ. That song never meant so much to me before I died as it does now.

You can be sure

When I talk to people I often ask them if they're married. If I were to ask you the same question, you would probably answer a quick yes or no. Then I'd ask you, "How do you know?"

Well, you'd probably refer back to the wedding when things became official and mention the wedding license. It's obvious, I realize.

But let's say that I ask you if you're a Christian. If you answer yes, I'll ask, "How do you know?"

"Well," you may say, "I know because I live a good life. I go to church often and am a member. I was baptized (or confirmed). I'm an elder, usher, or choir member. I give money to charity and the church."

Most people are sure about lots of things that affect their lives—like marriage—and can easily give the reasons they're so sure. But when I ask about something as important as eternal life, people are less certain.

That's sad because you *can* know for certain where you will spend eternity. You don't have to have a question in your mind about whether or not you're a Christian. You can know for sure.

God said there is only one way to be saved— Jesus Christ. He said, *I am the way—and the truth and the life. No one comes to the Father except through me* (John 14:6). So how do you accept Christ? Romans 10:9,10 says, *If you confess with your mouth, "Jesus is Lord," and believe in your heart that God raised him from the dead, you will be saved.* You can go to church and do good works, but if you have never been born into the spiritual kingdom of God, you are still lost, according to the Bible. *The gift of God is eternal life in Christ Jesus our Lord* (Romans 6:23).

God's Word teaches us that it is not the "good" people who go to heaven, because we are all sinners in God's view. It is the "forgiven" people who will spend eternity in His presence.

17

What will it cost you?

So what does it "cost" you to become a Christian? I've made a comparison to show you what you lose—and what you gain—by accepting Jesus Christ as your Lord and Savior.

What you give up when you become a Christian:

What you gain when you become a Christian:

Filthy rags
All of us have become like one who is unclean, and all our righteous acts are like filthy rags; we all shrivel up like a leaf, and like the wind our sins sweep us away (Isaiah 64:6).

Righteous robe
I delight greatly in the Lord; my soul rejoices in my God. For he has... arrayed me in a robe of righteousness, as a bridegroom adorns his head like a priest, and as a bride adorns herself with her jewels (Isaiah 61:10).

Worthlessness
"There is no one righteous, not even one; there is no one who... seeks God. All have turned away...[and] together become worthless; there is no one who does good, not even one" (Romans 3:10-12).

Godliness
His divine power has given us everything we need for life and godliness through our knowledge of him who called us by his own glory and goodness (2 Peter 1:3).

Poverty

What good is it for a man to gain the whole world, yet forfeit his soul? Or what can a man give in exchange for his soul? (Mark 8:36, 37).

Prosperity

For you know the grace of our Lord Jesus Christ, that though he was rich, yet for your sakes he became poor, so that you through his poverty might become rich (2 Corinthians 8,9).

Perplexity

"There will be signs in the sun, moon and stars. On the earth, nations will be in anguish and perplexity at the roaring and tossing of the sea. Men will faint from terror, apprehensive of what is coming on the world" (Luke 21:25,26).

Peace

"Peace I leave with you; my peace I give you. I do not give to you as the world gives. Do not let your hearts be troubled and do not be afraid" (John 14:27).

Death

For the wages of sin is death...

Eternal life

...but the gift of God is eternal life in Christ Jesus our Lord (Romans 6:23).

Judgment

Because of your stubbornness and your unrepentant heart, you are storing up wrath against yourself for the day of God's wrath,

Justification

Therefore, since we have been justified through faith, we have peace with God through our Lord Jesus Christ (Romans 5:1).

19

when his righteous judgment will be revealed (Romans 2:5).

Child of Satan
You belong to your father, the devil, and you want to carry out your father's desire (John 8:44).

Child of God
To all who received [Christ], to those who believed in his name, he gave the right to become children of God (John 1:12).

Destruction
Do no be deceived: God cannot be mocked. A man reaps what he sows. The one who sows to please his sinful nature, from that nature will reap destruction; the one who sows to please the Spirit, from the Spirit will reap eternal life (Galatians 6:7,8).

Deliverance
Since the children have flesh and blood, he too shared in their humanity so that by his death he might destroy him who holds the power of death—that is, the devil—and free those who all their lives were held in slavery by their fear of death (Hebrews 2:14, 15).

Hell
The wicked shall be turned into hell, and all the nations that forget God (Psalm 9:17, KJV).

Heaven
"Do not let your hearts be troubled. Trust in God; trust also in me. In my Father's house are many rooms; if it were not so, I would have told you. I am going there to prepare a place for you.

*And if I go and prepare
a place for you, I will
come back and take you
to be with me that you
also may be where I am"*
(John 14:1-3).

Why are so many willing to be satisfied with filthy rags, worthlessness, poverty, perplexity, death, judgment, Satan, destruction, and hell when they can have a robe of righteousness, godliness, prosperity, peace, eternal life, justification, God, deliverance, and heaven? Why feed on garbage when you can feast on the riches of God's grace?

Isaiah 1:18 says, *"Come now, let us reason together,"* says the Lord. *"Though your sins are like scarlet, they shall be as white as snow; though they are red as crimson, they shall be like wool."*

How can you obtain these things of God? When you accept the Lord as your personal Savior, your body becomes the temple of the Holy Spirit. His Spirit lives in you to help you grow spiritually. Just as your body needs air to live and grow, your spirit needs prayer and Bible study each day to live and grow.

Would you like a changed life before it is too late? You might not get a second chance, as I did. I urge you—accept Jesus Christ today!

Chapter 2

Hope and Prayer Working Together

An eyewitness account by Joe Cannavo

It was mid-afternoon, a mild sunny day. My wife, Emily, her friend Gloria, my son-in-law Nick, and I had just completed hitting a few baskets of golf balls. The others elected to finish up with a few shots at the putting green. I stayed behind to watch a few young boys from a local school practicing their driving skills with their coach.

As I turned to leave, I heard shouting behind me. I turned and saw someone lying across one of the mats. I first thought someone had been accidentally hit by a golf ball. I yelled at the woman inside the office to call for emergency assistance, and I raced over to see what had happened.

A gentleman (whose name I later found out was Bill Pew) was lying on his back, eyes open and breathing normally. I assumed he was conscious so I asked him, "Can you hear me? What's your name? Are you alone?" I got no response.

Several people gathered to help. One woman, Julie Sprague, knelt across from me. Julie, I later learned, was certified to administer CPR. Time seemed to stand still, and we all tried to decide how we could best assist Bill. One man produced a bottle of nitro-glycerin pills and suggested we give one to Bill. His breathing was beginning to be labored, so the man put one of his pills under Bill's tongue. As he tipped the bottle for another pill, he accidentally spilled all of them onto the grass.

Bill's breathing became more difficult, and after about five minutes, his breathing stopped! I was nearest Bill and began to apply chest pressure, and Julie began mouth-to-mouth resuscitation.

We thought we would get immediate results, but Bill made no response. After we had made a number of chest and breath applications, for a brief moment we almost revived him. He gave two or three breaths and then stopped again. Our hopes were dashed.

A few minutes later, my son-in-law came over and relieved me. Nick knows CPR, and he began working with Julie in CPR application.

I knelt along Bill's left side next to Nick and tried to take his pulse. I couldn't find one. I started praying to Jesus who is our Protector and Healer to spare this man and let him live. I could only think of his family. How terrible it would be if he were to die, so suddenly, so fast. I also prayed that God's will would be done. I was not the only one praying. Others around me were also praying that Bill would live.

Everything happening seemed unreal, and yet I felt calm. I never became nervous, upset, or extremely disturbed even though I believed the man was dying or already dead. I should have been shaken, but I wasn't. I continued to hold Bill's wrist, hoping and praying for even the slightest sign of a pulse. But there was none!

Twenty minutes or more passed, and the ambulance still had not arrived. We could hear it off in the distance. Nick and Julie continued the CPR, but time was running out. Why was it taking so long for the ambulance?

A bystander suggested that Bill might have special medical problems, so someone checked his wallet for any possible information. As Bill's wallet came out, I noticed the name "William." I began calling his name, "Bill, come on! Hang in there. You're going to make it." Suddenly, hope sprang up in all of us. It was as if we all knew "Bill." We began to call his name and encourage him—and ourselves. "C'mon, Bill. You can do it! The ambulance is almost here. Bill, don't give up!" It was beautiful—hope and prayer working together.

Finally, the medics arrived. They immediately began to administer oxygen to Bill, and they gave him a shot. Those of us who had been working on Bill moved away. At a distance, I observed the medics applying electric shocks at least five times to Bill's chest with no apparent success. They worked over him for a good five minutes, but nothing seemed to happen.

The medical team worked in such a rapid, thorough, serious, and efficient manner that they won my admiration. Because of my observations that day, I feel assured and extremely grateful that emergency teams like that one are available to help us in times of need.

The medics placed Bill into the ambulance, and it sped to the Naples Hospital. In the movies, ambulances always seem to almost fly, but it seemed to me the ambulance that day did not go very fast. I wondered if it was because the medics had arrived too late and that there wasn't any hope for Bill...no need to speed.

Those of us watching the ambulance drive away

were certain Bill would never make it. Nick shook his head and said, "That's a golfer's dream, I guess—to go while playing golf."

I firmly believe Jesus laid His hands on Bill that day. He returned him to his wonderful family and friends so he could enjoy life and continue to carry the good news of salvation to many more people. I give thanks to God Almighty for this miracle, and I am grateful to Him for the opportunity and privilege of being part of His workings in Bill's life that day. I also thank God for the chance to get to know a great and loving brother in Christ, Bill Pew!

Chapter 3

God's Plan For My Life

There's an old saying that hindsight is always better than foresight. I know that is true in my life. While I went through many interesting experiences growing up, I often didn't see God's hand working. It is only in looking back that I see clearly how He directed my life so completely.

In the beginning

I was born in Highland Park, Michigan, on August 21, 1922, and as a child was carried to church in my mother's arms. My family were committed churchgoers, and I accepted Christ when I was only seven years old.

My dad grew up in Canada. After serving in World War I, he moved to Michigan to work for Ford Motor Company, which was hiring veterans at $5.00 a day. Things were going well until 1930 when the Great Depression hit. Dad lost his job, home—everything—and we moved back to Canada to live on my granddad's farm.

I learned to work on that farm. I went to a one-room elementary school and when I graduated from there, I continued on in high school (a 10-mile bike ride every day). High school, however, was a complete disaster! We were required to complete four years of Latin and French, plus Canadian and British history. I couldn't see how these subjects would help me milk the cows and do the other work on the farm.

I took Latin and French my first year of high school and failed them both. I took them again the next year and failed again. I was so discouraged that I dropped out of school. Things were not going well on the farm. To help make ends meet, my dad returned to Detroit to find work. He got a job for the three months of winter, then he came home and worked for nine months on the farm.

One year Dad couldn't make it home for Christmas so I went to Detroit to stay with him. While there, a friend of Dad's told me that Excello, a large company in Detroit, was hiring. I applied right away and got a job making $3.00 an hour. What a lot of money that was! In Canada I had been working for only $1.00 a day, and now I was making $3.00 an hour as a messenger boy carrying communications from Engineering to the Front Office.

I discovered the value of money and a good education during my time at Excello. The engineers I worked with were making large sums of money— more than I ever dreamed a person could earn—and I knew I could do it, too.

Into the Navy

I was 19 years old and felt I was going to be called up for the draft, so one day I went down to the Federal Building to enlist in the Navy. I was standing in line when a Chief Petty Officer (a friend of my dad's) came up and asked me if I was Doyle Pew's son. I couldn't imagine how he knew me. He hadn't seen me for years and I didn't look like my dad, but somehow he picked me out. He asked me how good I was in mathematics. It was the one subject I had passed in school. I told him okay, and he took me to take an "Eddy" test. If I passed, I could enlist in the Navy as a Third Class Petty Officer and the Navy would send me to school to learn radio and radar.

I took the test and a week later was accepted for radar school. After basic training, I was sent to Texas A & M to study the fundamentals of electricity. I was now eager to learn. I passed the course and was sent to Ward Island in Corpus Christi, Texas, for training in radar. I studied very hard and passed with flying colors. In fact, I did so well the Navy kept me as an instructor.

One day the commander of my base came to me and asked if he could attend my class. He said he wanted to learn about radar, and he promised not to ask any questions during the class. He asked if I would stay after class to answer any questions he might have. I didn't have anything else to do, so I gladly consented. And I enjoyed teaching him the principles involved in making a line go around a screen and causing an image to appear.

One day I saw a notice on the bulletin board that said the Navy was going to pick 12 men from my camp to send to college as part of a special program called "V12." I knew my chances for being one of the 12 were very small. First, my naval district in Corpus Christi was very large, with thousands of personnel, as it was the largest training center for Navy pilots. Second, many of the sailors there already had one or two years of college. Third, only high school graduates could apply.

I ignored all of this and applied. I took several tests which eliminated many of the applicants, and finally it came down to a personal interview. I walked in the room where the selection committee of commanders was sitting, and there was my commander. He looked at me and told me I was excused.

In a couple of weeks the names of the 12 lucky people were posted. My name was last on the list. I had to send for my high school records and my supposed "diploma." I didn't know what to do. I wrote a letter to the principal of the high school I had attended, and he wrote me a very nice letter back. Unfortunately, he also attached my records. They were a total disaster! I had failed almost every subject and never got past my second year.

A week later, my commander asked me if I was getting the necessary papers together to attend college. I had to tell him that I never got through high school, and I showed him my records. I quickly added that I was sure if I got the chance to go to college I could make it.

My commander was pretty disgusted with me. He told me that I shouldn't have applied for the training if I didn't have a high school diploma. He left and, about three hours later, I got a message to report to headquarters. My commander had a jeep ready and we went into Corpus Christi. He took me to a high school where we met the principal who talked with me and asked me questions. When we left, I had my diploma!

I was sent to Louisiana Tech for my first two years of training and was on the honor roll. In fact, my parents even received a letter (which I still have today) informing them of my great progress. Then I was sent to Rice University in Houston, Texas, for my last two years of training in electrical engineering. I remained on the honor roll all the way through college.

The war ended and I was discharged. When I arrived back in Detroit, I went into the electronics business, designing and building control panels for transfer machines and automation. This was a new field, and within a short time I was doing a considerable amount of work for the automobile manufacturers and making a good living. In fact, I was making more money than I ever dreamed possible.

God worked in my life

Why am I telling you all this? To show you how God worked in my life. And if He would consent to work in my life, I know He will do the same for anyone who loves and serves Him.

Here are some of the ways I know God has worked in my life:

1. My family took me to church regularly, beginning when I was only a small baby. From that, a good spiritual foundation was laid in my life.

2. When Dad lost his job and we had to move to my granddad's farm, it seemed like a tragedy. I know now that it was one of the best things that happened to me because I learned how to work hard and the value of hard work.

3. When I went to work at Excello in Detroit, I got a first-hand look at what education could do for a person. I realized how valuable education is and got a real desire to learn.

4. When the Chief Petty Officer picked me out of the Navy enlistment line-up that day and had me take the "Eddy" test, it was the start of my electrical train-

ing. I know now that bumping into him that day was not a coincidence—it was God working in my life.

5. When I attended the radio and radar school at Texas A&M, I found out that, through hard work, I could do as well as anyone.

6. I was chosen out of thousands to attend college through the V12 program, in large part, because my commander knew me and was on the selection committee. With his help, I received a college education and the start of a new life.

7. I had the opportunity to attend Louisiana Tech and Rice University—two well-known institutions—to study for a career in electrical engineering, a field that was just then in great demand.

8. I arrived back in Detroit after my discharge from the Navy at just the right time. The automobile makers needed automation machines and I had the know-how to help them. God timed everything just right to make my life successful in business.

When I look back on all the things that changed my life, a lot of people deserve credit for helping make me what I am today. But mostly Jesus Christ deserves the credit and praise. He was opening and closing the doors in my life and bringing about events over which I had no control. I give Him all the praise and glory, and I thank Him that He never lets me take the credit.

The ups and downs

I wish I could say that I have been as consistent in my Christian life as God was in His dealings with me, but I can't. For the most part, my Christian life has been one of ups and downs. I attended church. I always gave at least ten percent of my earnings to

God. But I wasn't as committed as I should have been.

I am so thankful that God is so much more merciful and patient than we are. Even when I dropped dead at the age of 65— which seemed at the moment to be the greatest tragedy of my life He restored my life and turned my greatest tragedy into my greatest triumph. He allowed me to see life differently, to change my priorities and goals. Today, serving the Lord and pointing others to Him is the most important thing in the world to me. I witness to every person I can, even at the risk of being called a religious fanatic.

Am I a "fanatic"?

Webster's Dictionary defines *fanaticism* as "excessive enthusiasm and often intense uncritical devotion." I understand what it means because I used to be a sports fanatic.

Several years ago my company had several seats for the Detroit Red Wings hockey games. I knew several Red Wings players personally, including Red Kelly and his wife, Johnny Wilson, Gordie Howe, Marty Pavelich, and others. My wife and Red Kelly are from the same district in Canada, so we became good friends and often gathered with the team after their games.

I never missed a Red Wings game. When the team was playing, I would move with their every play—check, shoot, etc. I felt like I was playing with them, so much so that at the end of the games I would be covered with perspiration and emotionally charged.

I was a fanatic. After a game I would talk hockey to my customers, family, and friends. I lived, breathed, and ate hockey. It was all I could think about. Yet, a few days after a game I would run out of things to say.

The game was old news and no one wanted to talk about it. The joy of the game was gone, so I would start thinking about the next game. And then the cycle would repeat itself from game to game throughout the season and playoffs.

The Stanley Cup Playoffs was the highlight of the year for me. I was ecstatic. My life was wrapped up in these games and most everything else didn't matter while they were going on. I'm sure my friends got tired of hearing me talk hockey, but they didn't complain. They just called me a great sport, a real hockey fan.

When the season was finally over, I couldn't wait for the new season to begin. Hockey was the most important thing in my life. I was a Christian, yes, but I made very little time for the spiritual things that would last forever. I probably didn't spend more than an hour a week on them.

Unfortunately, there are a lot of people like I was. Their lives are totally wrapped up in baseball, football, soap operas, rock groups, etc. They are fanatics. Their lives revolve around their team, group, or show. No one thinks anything about 60,000 or more people attending a sports event or rock concert, even in adverse weather. And people will go to all kinds of lengths to prove their devotion, even so far as making fools of themselves on national television before millions of viewers. But we don't think anything about it. They're just good fans, that's all.

I have friends who play golf 3 to 5 days a week, 4 to 5 hours each day. That's 15 to 20 hours a week. Yet, a week later these games are history and most will never be thought of again. But no one considers people like these fanatics. They're simply great fans of the game.

And what if a neighbor asks you to play a game of golf with him at his club or offers you a ticket to a sporting event? Wouldn't you consider the neighbor a good, thoughtful friend? Yet, often when I try to talk to someone for just five minutes about Jesus Christ and salvation, I am promptly branded a religious fanatic, especially if I invite the person to attend Bible study or church with me.

Why the difference? Spending 20 hours a week on a sporting event or television program is judged by the world as being a good fan. Yet, spending 5 minutes a week to discuss spiritual things that could mean eternal life or death for someone is judged by the world as fanatical.

First John 3:1 says, *How great is the love the Father has lavished on us, that we should be called children of God!* And that is what we are! The reason the world does not know us is that it did not know Him. Your non-Christian friends don't understand your witness because they don't know God. In Luke 21:17 Jesus warned His followers, *All men will hate you because of me.*

In John 15:18-21, Jesus explains why the world hates us. *"If the world hates you, keep in mind that it hated me first. If you belonged to the world, it would love you as its own. As it is, you do not belong to the world, but I have chosen you out of the world. That is why the world hates you. Remember the words I spoke to you: 'No servant is greater than his master.' If they persecuted me, they will persecute you also. If they obeyed my teaching, they will obey yours also. They will treat you this way because of my name, for they do not know the One who sent me."*

The Bible says everything will some day pass away, but the truth of God will never pass away (see

Matthew 24:35). So why then do we spend hours on worldly things that will pass away and spend so little time each day doing the things that will last forever—praying, studying God's Word, witnessing?

I've done a lot of exciting things in my life. I have managed a large, successful business, and collected big game trophies in the northwest and Alaska. That was exciting.

I dearly love my wife and family, and that is exciting.

I killed a Kodiak bear in the dark of night as he was tearing a meat house apart. Knowing I was just a few jumps away from a dying bear was really exciting. And when I fell through a glacier bank and dangled precariously over a roaring river fifty feet below until—miraculously—I was saved, that was exciting!

Later on, when I had a large section of my chest removed to rid my body of a deadly, rapidly-spreading melanoma cancer, I had a definite sense of exhilaration. My doctor told me that I beat certain death by the narrowest of margins.

But none of these things compare with the thrill of knowing that Jesus Christ is living within me. Every human achievement or experience pales in comparison with having a personal relationship with the eternal Son of God.

No problem or situation can worry me now. My life is fuller than ever and it has real purpose. I know where I have been. I know where I am now, and I know beyond any doubt where I am going. *Whoever believes in the Son has eternal life* (John 3:36). Every believer in Jesus Christ has eternal life now. If you are in doubt about whether you do or not, there is a good chance that you have never made this personal commitment. It would be tragic to find out after death that you do NOT have eternal life.

Oh, how I wish I had gone through my experience with death years ago before I had wasted so much valuable time on meaningless things. Now, I've been given a second chance and my priorities have changed. My brush with eternity has made me aware of what really matters in this life.

I have a second chance, but you might not get one. I pray that the things I have learned will make a difference in your life. Please consider what your priorities are today. Are you spending your life on the things that really matter? Are you preparing for eternity?

You have a choice. What kind of fanatic will you be...temporal or eternal?

Chapter 4

Knowing the Will of God

One of the most important things a Christian can do is to obey the will of God, and you can't obey His will until you know what His will is. It's easy as a Christian to look back at your life and see how God led you, but it's sometimes difficult in the present to know what God's will is.

Yet, God's Word tells us how important it is that we do His will. First John 2:17 says, *The world and its desires pass away, but the man who does the will of God lives forever.* That's a pretty good incentive to do God's will.

So what is God's will for you? Before you can understand what His will is, you must be a Christian and realize that He has a plan for your life. Ephesians 2:10 says, *For we are God's workmanship, created in Christ Jesus to do good works, which God prepared in advance for us to do.*

Trust in the Lord with all your heart, says Proverbs 3:5,6, *and lean not on your own understanding; in all your ways acknowledge him, and he will make your paths straight.*

God has revealed His will

Throughout the Bible, God has revealed His will for your life. Some of His do's and don'ts include the Ten Commandments, the teachings of Jesus, and what the authors of the New Testament have declared as God's will. You don't have to pray for God to reveal His will in these areas. You just have to study the Scriptures and make them a part of your life.

Some other important things God wants for you are in this list by John Debrine:

1. It is God's will that you dedicate your life to Him (Romans 12:1,2).

2. It is God's will that all people be saved (2 Peter 3:9) and that you are involved in reaching people for Christ (Matthew 28:19,20).

3. It is God's will that you be spiritually self-sustaining (1 Thessalonians 5:18).

4. It is God's will that you live a life according to Christ's standards and not the standards of the world (1 Thessalonians 4:3-8).

5. It is God's will that you handle difficulty through His Word (1 Peter 2:20,21).

6. It is God's will that you grow spiritually (Ephesians 4:1-16).

7. It is God's will that you recognize that you will go through good times and bad times as you obey Him (1 Peter 4:12-19).

8. It is God's will that you don't follow your sinful nature (Galatians 6:7-9) but rather the Holy Spirit (1 Peter 4:2).

Every day we have the choice of letting the Holy Spirit guide our lives or to follow our sinful nature (compare Romans 6:13 and 8:13 which teach about this choice). When we let the Holy Spirit guide our lives and live to please God instead of ourselves, God has promised us abundant life. In John 10:10 (KJV) Jesus says, *I am come that they might have life, and that they might have it more abundantly.*

The Bible also tells us about the things we shouldn't do. For example, in 2 Corinthians 6:14-18 God tells us not to marry unbelievers. Christians are NOT to marry non-Christians. There is no room for discussion on the matter. You don't have to pray and ask God what His will is on this matter. He has already declared in His Word that a Christian should never marry someone who isn't a Christian.

There are other don'ts in God's Word that we are to obey. God's will in many situations is clearly spelled out in the Bible. That's why it's so important that we study God's Word and ask for His guidance in daily prayer. It's a day-by-day journey.

When the Bible doesn't say

Of course, there are many situations we encounter in life about which the Bible says nothing. What do we do then? How can we find God's will for those situations?

Being human, we would like God to give us a complete map of our lifetimes so we would know exactly what His will is for us in every circumstance. But God doesn't work that way. He wants us to take one day at a time and follow Him. Jesus said, *"Do not worry about tomorrow, for tomorrow will worry about itself. Each day has enough trouble of its own"* (Matthew 6:34).

The secret of knowing God's will is to know God. How do we do that? By practicing spiritual breathing. We take the goodness of God into our lives through prayer and Bible study and we let Him expel the

41

badness of sin. As we become more like Jesus, we can find and do His will more easily.

You can't go just by your feelings—"I just FEEL this is what God wants me to do." Feelings will let you down. They'll confuse you and lead you astray. You have to go by God's Word and your knowledge of Him—and THEN your feelings can confirm what you know.

There's another source of help in learning to know God better. It's the committed, faithful people of God around you. Listen to their advice. Read their books. Watch their lives. And let the Holy Spirit work through their counsel and teachings.

God's will isn't always easy

Now, a lot of people seem to think that walking in God's will means we will never have any trouble, but that's not true. Jesus said, *"If the world hates you, keep in mind that it hated me first. If you belonged to the world, it would love you as its own. As it is, you do not belong to the world, but I have chosen you out of the world. That is why the world hates you. Remember the words I spoke to you: 'No servant is greater than his master.' If they persecuted me, they will persecute you also"* (John 15:18-20).

Problems will come for each of us. The good news is, when we walk in God's will He will turn the bad into good. Romans 8:28 says, *We know that in all things God works for the good of those who love him, who have been called according to his purpose.*

Verses 31-39 of that chapter goes on to say: *If God is for us, who can be against us? He who did not spare his own Son, but gave him up for us all—how will he not also, along with him, graciously give us all things? Who will bring any charge against those*

*whom God has chosen? It is God who justifies. Who
is he that condemns? Christ Jesus, who died—more
than that, who was raised to life—is at the right hand
of God and is also interceding for us.*

*Who shall separate us from the love of Christ?
Shall trouble or hardship or persecution or famine or
nakedness or danger or sword? As it is written: "For
your sake we face death all day long; we are considered as sheep to be slaughtered." No, in all these
things we are more than conquerors through him who
loved us.*

*For I am convinced that neither death nor life,
neither angels nor demons, neither the present nor the
future, nor any powers, neither height nor depth, nor
anything else in all creation, will be able to separate
us from the love of God that is in Christ Jesus our
Lord.*

When you love God and do His will, NOTHING
can separate you from Him. No problem is bigger
than God's love and grace. The world, the flesh, and
the devil will try to hinder you from following God's
will, but you'll have help from God, Jesus Christ, and
the Holy Spirit. And you and I both know which side
is stronger!

Every day I ask God to show me what He wants
me to do. Sure, I make mistakes. I am a Christian,
but I am still in the flesh. When I do fail, however, I
know who I can turn to—Jesus Christ.

The greatest commandment

Doing the will of God often seems to be confusing to us, but Jesus summed it all up when He told the
Pharisees what the greatest commandment is. He
said, *"'Love the Lord your God with all your heart
and with all your soul and with all your mind and with*

all your strength.' The second is this: 'Love your neighbor as yourself.' There is no greater commandment than these" (Mark 12:30,31).

When we passionately love God with everything we are, it is easy to know His will and obey Him. We need to love Him with our hearts, our souls, our minds, and our strength. When we base our relationship with God on intellect alone, we fall into the trap of having to understand everything. We need proof in order to believe. When we base our relationship with God on our feelings, we are easily led into error. We have no real basis on which to stand. Paul described people like this. He said, *Jews demand miraculous signs and Greeks look for wisdom, but we preach Christ crucified: a stumbling block to Jews and foolishness to Gentiles* (1 Corinthians 1:22,23). We must serve God with both our hearts and our heads.

Serving God without involving our souls is merely obeying tradition. We go to church and participate in the traditions of the church because we were raised to do so, but there is no personal commitment on our part. Unfortunately, going to church will never get us into heaven. We must make a personal commitment to Jesus Christ in order to be saved.

When we serve God, Jesus said, we must also serve Him with all our strength. I think that means absolute resolve and physical involvement. We purpose to serve God no matter what, and we get physically involved in serving Him. We don't sit back on our padded church pews and watch the world go by. We're like the Good Samaritan in Luke 10:25-37. We go out into the highways and byways of our world to help the poor, the homeless, the needy, the lost and bring them to God.

You can know the will of God—from His Word,

from your personal relationship with Him, and from other Christians. And when you obey His will, your life will be more fruitful and more abundant in His love.

Chapter 5

The Most Important Book in the World

After coming back from death, I've had an over-whelming realization of how holy and powerful God really is, and I have a desire to know Him better. Christ came to our world, sinless and perfect, died for our sins, was buried, and rose from the dead to live forever. When He returned to heaven, He sent His Holy Spirit to live in all those who accept Him.

Because I have such a great desire to know and understand God and His Word, I find it difficult to understand why people will so quickly believe a lie like evolution instead of the truth of creation by God as written in His Word. I fervently believe the Bible is the most important book in the world.

Why? Because it is the only written word given to us by God. In America we have Bibles everywhere. Yet, tragically, the majority of people know almost nothing of what the Bible says. They don't read it, and the majority of those who do fail to apply its truths to their lives.

Our nation is searching for answers to the world's problems. How tragic that there are suffering, unsatisfied people all around us while the answers and help they need is right at their fingertips. The Bible has the Answer for every problem that exists. Jesus Christ said, *"I am the way and the truth and the life. No one comes to the Father except through me "*(John 14:6).

Only Jesus can give you peace in this life and for all eternity. You won't find the answers to your problems in the world's wisdom. The Bible says, *Do not deceive yourselves. If any one of you thinks he is wise by the standards of this age, he should become a "fool" so that he may become wise. For the wisdom of this world is foolishness in God's sight. As it is written: "He catches the wise in their craftiness" ; and again, "The Lord knows that the thoughts of the wise are futile"* (1 Corinthians 3:18-20).

God says that worldly knowledge is foolishness to Him, and I believe it now more than ever. The worldly scholars cannot tell you where man came from, why we are here, and what is going to happen to us after death. But God's Word can. The Bible tells us that all things were made by God for His pleasure and glory. It tells us that we are separated from God by our sin and the only way back to God is through Jesus Christ. Through Jesus we can have abundant life in this world and in the world after death.

Why should you read the Bible?

This is why it is so important that we read the Bible. It tells us about God and what He expects of us. It tells us the way of salvation. The Bible also teaches that we must be able to explain salvation to those who are searching for answers to their problems (see 1 Peter 3:15). This is God's commandment and our duty.

Our faith also comes from reading the Bible (see Romans 10:17). By using God's Word as our standard and guide, we can determine what is true and what is false teaching. It is our road map to keep us on the narrow way that leads to God. The influence of the world is very strong, and it is only by knowing the Word of God that we can escape its pull.

The greatest reason to read and study the Bible is to know God better. His Word tells us what He is really like—what He loves and hates, what makes Him happy and sad, what angers Him and pleases Him. The Bible is really one long love story of how God made us and loved us so much that He sent His Son to die for us. And it tells us that someday He is coming back to take us to heaven where we will live "happily ever after."

Why I believe in the Bible

I've heard many convincing arguments about why the Bible is really God's Word. For me, one of the most convincing is the way it has stood the test of time. In all the writings of other religions you will not find a single prediction made by their writers that has come true. Buddha could not prophesy the future. Mohammed's writings are filled with confusion. Yet, the Bible is full of prophecies throughout the Old and New Testaments that have already come true. Can you imagine the odds of that happening by chance?

For example, consider the life of Jesus. Thousands of years before Jesus was born, the Old Testament writers told where He would be born, that His family would flee to Egypt, that His own people would reject Him, that He would be crucified and would raise from the dead. And every prophecy came true! How is that possible? Only because the eternal God of the universe inspired men to write the prophecies just as He knew they would later happen.

49

Our human minds are not capable of knowing the future. Sometimes people say they feel "premonitions" about things that are about to happen. And we might have a lucky guess once in a while. But the chances of anyone making predictions and those predictions consistently coming true are very small.

Back in the fifties and early sixties, the press gave a lot of coverage to Jeanne Dixon, a "prophetess" who predicted the future. I remember on one particular occasion she was asked to predict who would win in the national primary elections. When the primaries were over, the winners were compared with Jeanne's predictions. She wasn't even close—she had missed every one!

The latest "prophetess" in the press nowadays is Shirley MacLaine. So many Americans are willing to turn their backs on God and His proven Word and follow someone like Shirley MacLaine and the New Age Movement. This broad coalition of neo-Hindu airheads, with Miss MacLaine as their symbolic guru, has captured a large group of the entertainment, cultural, and jet-set leadership of our country. They eagerly follow her predictions and leadership.

Miss MacLaine says God is all and all is God, and she stretches her arms out and proclaims that she is God. She tells about her "past lives" and makes predictions about the future, but very few of them come true. How sad that people are content to follow a person like Miss MacLaine, who has led an immoral, self-centered life, when they could follow the most loving, forgiving, self-sacrificing person who ever lived, Jesus Christ.

Every day we hear predictions of things that are supposed to happen, and except for a few lucky guesses, most of them are wrong. Yet God's Word has never been proven wrong. For centuries men have devoted their entire lifetimes to trying to find just one error in its pages and, after many years of searching, have declared the Word of God to be accurate and true.

Science proves the truth of God's Word

Even science, which for years regarded the Bible as fiction, has never been able to disprove God's Word. In fact, year after year, scientists have confirmed its truths. The One who wrote the Bible said, *"I am the Alpha* [beginning] *and the Omega* [end]," *says the Lord God, "who is, and who was, and who is to come, the Almighty"* (Revelation 1:8). The psalmist wrote, *Lord, you have been our dwelling place throughout all generations. Before the mountains were born or you brought forth the earth and the world, from everlasting to everlasting you are God* (Psalm 90:1,2).

The Bible says, *The heavens declare the glory of God; the skies proclaim the work of his hands* (Psalm 19:1), and science has confirmed that. Astronomers tell us that if our planet were any closer to the sun it would burn up, and if it were any further away it would be covered with ice. What are the chances that our planet just "happened" to be in the right position to support life?

The human body is one of the greatest proofs of God's existence in our world. Psalm 139:14 says, I *praise you* [God] *because I am fearfully and wonderfully made.* Every organ in our bodies, our eyes, our noses, our bone structures and nervous systems—everything about us is miraculous! How can intelligent people possibly believe that we simply came into being by chance, that we just happened to evolve from slime in some swamp somewhere? How much easier to believe that a loving God made us in His image for His glory.

Our circulation system is one of the greatest miracles of our bodies. Our blood courses through our bodies for more than 60,000 miles—that's enough to circle the globe two and a half times. As it travels, it services one hundred trillion inhabitants, living cells that form and make us. Everything we need to sustain our bodies is brought to the individual cells by the blood: oxygen, nutrients, water, disease fighters.

The body normally produces two million or more red blood cells every second to replace those damaged by the rigors of circulation.

Our hearts send blood cells to our toes and back to our hearts in less than 30 seconds. Some of this delivery route is so narrow that the cells must be sent in single file in order to get through.

The heart itself weighs less than a pound and is smaller than your fist. It has four one-way valves, each of them as thin as a sheet of paper, yet more durable than an iron hinge. Each opens and closes to precise specifications which control where the blood will go in the body.

Under normal conditions, the human heart will pump about five quarts of blood every minute. In a day, that total can exceed 1,800 gallons of blood, and in an average lifetime, it can exceed more than 55 million gallons or enough to fill a string of tank cars 50 miles long.

The blood is the cleanser of the body. Blood cells travel down capillaries one-tenth the diameter of a human hair. There they are stripped of their food and oxygen and loaded with carbon dioxide and urea. The cells are then sent to the kidneys to release their waste and then to the lungs to exchange the carbon dioxide for oxygen before starting their journey all over again.

(And just as our blood cleanses the body of wastes, so the blood Jesus Christ shed for us cleanses us spiritually from sin.)

This is only part of the miracle that we are. Can you really believe that we were created by evolutionary forces, by chance? Or can you see how impossible that would be, and that we were created by God and Him alone?

Atheists may face life and death with a smile and an arrogant attitude, but I believe that deep inside they would like to have the faith that only Jesus Christ can give. They must long for a promise of life after death instead of a grave, the assurance of an eternity in the presence of God instead of the nothingness of non-existence.

My belief in the infallibility of the Bible has given me a much greater love for God. In this time of growing atheism, drug use, homosexual acceptance, and blatant rejection and mockery of the life of Jesus, I have peace in knowing that God is in control. And someday, the Bible says, *that at the name of Jesus every knee* [shall] *bow, in heaven and on earth and under the earth, and every tongue confess that Jesus Christ is Lord, to the glory of God the Father* (Philippians 2:10,11).

You must have a personal belief

It is this growing rejection of Jesus Christ and His Word that has spiritually blinded so many and caused the tidal wave of sin that is destroying America today. Many say they believe in God, but just a belief is not enough. You must personally ask Jesus Christ to forgive your sins. You must believe that He died on a cross for your salvation.

The Bible says, *If you confess with your mouth, "Jesus is Lord," and believe in your heart that God raised him from the dead, you will be saved. For it is with your heart that you believe and are justified, and it is with your mouth that you confess and are saved* (Romans 10:9,10).

That scripture confirms that if you accept Jesus as your Savior and Lord, He will forgive you of your sins and give you eternal life. He will wash away the past and give you a brand-new life.

I know now what really matters

Can you understand why my priorities changed after my sudden cardiac death? Suddenly I understood what is really important in this life. The only things that matter are our souls and our relationship with God. So many people care more for their cars and possessions than they do about their souls and where they are going to spend eternity.

Since my experience, my life has been radically changed. I have a greater appreciation of life and a greater tolerance and compassion for others. I am less concerned with material goods, status, and how I appear to others. I have lost all fear of death. I feel I am much closer to God than I was. I now realize that religion is man-made but Christianity is God-made. It's a waste of time to get tangled up in religious debates and traditions because they aren't really that important. What's truly important is Jesus Christ. He said, *"I am the way and the truth and the life. No one comes to the Father except through me"* (John 14:6).

Before I died, I lived a "normal" Christian life. I loved God, went to church, but still had too much sin in my life. Now, however, I want to tell everybody what life means and how they can be sure where they will spend eternity. I want to tell them that the Bible has the answers they need. I feel like I've been hit with something greater than myself. I've been given a second chance.

I've been changed because I died and came back to life, but anyone can change without actually experiencing what I did. The greatness of God's love is available to anyone. James 4:8 says, *Come near to God and he will come near to you.*

The things I once valued most in life are worthless to me now. The things I once thought were of little value are now the most important things in my life. The things I thought I would never do I am now doing. I have found that nothing is more important in life than our relationship with God. Financial security, a good job, good health, good family relationships—all these are important. Yet, they are only temporary unless we have a spiritual relationship with God.

After my million-to-one encounter with death, I felt like Lazarus, walking away from the grave into a new life, completely changed from the past. Of course, things haven't been perfect. I can't do some of the things I used to do. My short-term memory has been defective. My tolerance of emotional stress has been greatly reduced. But I also have a much more positive outlook on life. Every hour of every day is a bonus. Even for the small things that happen each day—good and bad—I say, "Thank You, God!"

Death has so much more meaning to me now. After my brother's sudden death last year, I realized again how we are lost forever to life on this earth when we go on that final walk with death. I don't know when or where, but I do know for sure that I will have another meeting with death and I will probably walk from that one in the opposite direction. I'm not afraid. Time is not an enemy now, but every moment is a priceless gift from God.

The best part of my "new" life is that God has opened the doors for me, through the Holy Spirit, to tell others of the great love of Christ. Because of my experience, I have been able to share with many people I wouldn't otherwise have had the opportunity to witness to. I am now truly a blessed and happy man!

My experience reminds me of a story about a man who was fishing on the Niagara River.

He was boating a few miles up from the falls, which he frequently did. But one day out on the river, his boat motor stopped and he started drifting with the current. He was not concerned at first. He just kept pulling on the starting cord. But the motor wouldn't start.

As he drifted and worked with the motor, he heard a great roar off in the distance and realized he was getting close to Niagara Falls. He worked frantically, but to no avail. The roar of the falls got louder and louder. Soon he could even see the mist rising from the falls, and the current was rushing his boat faster and faster toward the brink.

When he was only 200 feet away, the man realized his time had come. Nothing could be done even if the motor started.

Then, above the roar of the falls, he heard a faint engine noise over his head. He looked up and there was a helicopter hovering over him, a long rope hanging down from its open door. He grabbed the rope just as his boat started its plunge over the falls. He held on tight and the helicopter flew to the bank

56

where it slowly let him down until his feet touched solid ground.

The man dropped to his knees and thanked God for this "miracle" which saved his life. The experience completely changed his attitude about life and death.

Does this illustration represent your life as you are traveling through the river of life, with no plans for eternity, and the falls getting closer all the time? It will soon be time for you to go over the brink of life.

If I was walking along the banks of the Niagara River and saw someone getting close to the falls, I would not just stand there and watch. No—I would put my hands up to my mouth and shout as loud as I could, "Stop, turn around and change your course. You are heading the wrong way!"

So I now tell everyone who will listen that death is just up the road. Are you prepared for that moment? I cannot be content to see you on a course where you have no assurance of eternity with Christ. God can give you this assurance. *These things have I written unto you that believe on the name of the Son of God; that ye may know that ye have eternal life* (1 John 5:13, KJV).

Please let my experience be your experience and be prepared when God says "Come home." You will not be too busy to die. And only the commitment you have made with God will determine where you will spend eternity. Shouldn't you consider this before it's too late? Do it now while you still have a choice.

Chapter 6

The Laws of the Universe

When God created the heavens and the earth, He established physical laws to govern the physical universe. Everyone knows about the law of gravity. If you jump out of a ten-story building, you will fall down, not up. There are laws governing mathematics and science, and laws governing health.

There are laws of nature which cannot be violated without disaster. They are fixed and precise. For example, we can calculate to the minute when the sun will come up on a morning years in the future. The laws of nature determine such things as the tilt of the earth which gives us our seasons. Too much tilt one way or the other and we would either burn up from the heat of the sun or freeze from the cold of space.

God created and controls these exacting laws that govern our everyday lives. Colossians 1:15-17 says, [Jesus] *is the image of the invisible God, the firstborn over all creation. For by him all things were created: things in heaven and on earth, visible and invisible, whether thrones or powers or rulers or authorities; all things were created by him and for him. He is before all things, and in him all things hold together.*

To believe that all creation happened by chance is absurd. Only a rational, ordered being (God) could establish these laws millions of years ago, laws that continue to hold the universe together today. Every year we discover new laws about the universe that have existed since the beginning of time.

Romans 1:18-20 says, *The wrath of God is being revealed from heaven against all the godlessness and wickedness of men who suppress the truth by their wickedness, since what may be known about God is plain to them, because God has made it plain to them. For since the creation of the world God's invisible qualities—his eternal power and divine nature—have been clearly seen, being understood from what has been made, so that men are without excuse.*

God has put His handprint so clearly and indelibly upon creation that only a fool would refuse to see and accept it. God says that those who do will be without excuse on that great day when they stand before Him.

For centuries, people have tried to wipe God out of their lives. The Bible describes them this way: *For although they knew God, they neither glorified him as God nor gave thanks to him, but their thinking became futile and their foolish hearts were darkened. Although they claimed to be wise, they became fools* (Romans 1:21,22).

But the truth is, we can't wipe God out of our lives. Even in our sinful culture, we are surrounded by reminders of Jesus Christ. Every time a person writes a month, day, and year, he is acknowledging the existence of Christ. Our calendar and dating system are centered on the life of Jesus. The years before Jesus was born are designated B.C. or *Before Christ.*

60

The years after his birth are A.D. or *Anno Domini* which means "in the year of our Lord."

All over the world, people of all religions and nationalities use this dating system that testifies to the life, death, and resurrection of Jesus. Without realizing it, they are proclaiming that Jesus really did live on this earth. Is there any other person who ever lived in the world so recognized and validated as this?

The Four Spiritual Laws

Just as there are physical laws that govern your life, there are also spiritual laws which govern your relationship with God. My good friend, Bill Bright, of Campus Crusade For Christ, calls these "The Four Spiritual Laws." I have never found a better explanation of God's love, man's sin, Christ, and salvation than that found in these four simple laws.

Law One:

God loves you and has a wonderful plan for your life.

The Bible, God's special book to mankind, says: *For God so loved the world, that he gave his only begotten Son, that whosoever believeth in him should not perish, but have everlasting life* (John 3:16, KJV).

God's Son, Jesus, willingly made the ultimate sacrifice of himself so we could have a fulfilling life. He said, *I am come that they might have life, and that they might have it more abundantly* (John 10:10, KJV).

As I see it, that's great news. God has already shown that He loves us. There can be no doubt about that since He gave His sinless, one-of-a-kind Son for the entire human race. But there's some bad news I've got to tell you about.

61

Law Two:

Man is sinful and separated from God. There-fore, we cannot know and experience God's love and plan on our own. *For all have sinned, and come short of the glory of God* (Romans 3:23, KJV).

The original man and woman were created to have fellowship with God. But because of their own stubborn self-will, they chose independence, breaking the close friendship they had enjoyed with God. That same self-will we have today, characterized by an attitude of either active rebellion or passive indiffer-ence. The Bible calls it sin. The Bible says, *For the wages of sin is death* [spiritual separation from God] (Romans 6:23, KJV).

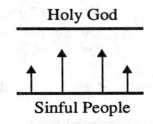

Holy God

Sinful People

This diagram illustrates what I mean. God is holy and man is sinful. The Bible makes it clear that no matter how hard we try, we can never reclaim that friendship with God or gain forgiveness by our own efforts.

Law Three:

Jesus Christ is God's only provision for man's sin. Through Him you can know and experience God's love and plan for your life, just as I have.

Jesus died in our place. *God demonstrates his own love for us in this: While we were still sinners, Christ died for us* (Romans 5:8).

I'm happy to report that the relationship I keep talking about is with a living Christ. He died for us by shedding His blood and was buried. But Jesus came back to life three days later, having conquered death. Over 500 people witnessed the resurrected Christ before He returned to heaven (see 1 Corinthians 15:3-6). He proved that the kind of life He offers is stronger than physical death.

But there's only one way to obtain that eternal life and find forgiveness for our sins. Jesus put it best when He said, *"I am the way and the truth and the life. No one comes to the Father except through me"* (John 14:6).

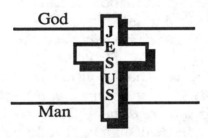

This diagram illustrates how God bridged the gulf that separates us from Him by sending His Son, Jesus Christ, to die on the cross to pay the penalty for our sins. Jesus defeated sin and death and rose from the grave. It isn't enough to just know these facts—Law Four explains what we must do to become a child of God.

Law Four:

You must individually receive Jesus Christ as Savior and Lord of your life. It requires a total commitment by faith in Him. Contrary to what a lot of people believe, it's not a matter of belonging to a church or having Christian parents or trying to live a good life. You must receive Him as your Savior by your own personal decision.

When you truly believe—trust—in Christ's death for you, God promises that *to all who received him, to those who believed in his name, he gave the right to become children of God* (John 1:12). Then you can know and experience God's love and plan for yourself, just as I have.

You must receive Christ through faith. *For it is by grace you have been saved, through faith—and this not from yourselves, it is the gift of God—not by works, so that no one can boast* (Ephesians 2:8,9).

When you receive Christ, you experience a new birth. John 3:1-5 tells about a man named Nicodemus who experienced a new birth. *Now there was a man of the Pharisees named Nicodemus, a member of the Jewish ruling council. He came to Jesus at night and said, "Rabbi, we know you are a teacher who has come from God. For no one could perform the miraculous signs you are doing if God were not with him."*

In reply Jesus declared, "I tell you the truth, unless a man is born again, he cannot see the kingdom of God."

"How can a man be born when he is old?" Nicodemus asked. "Surely he cannot enter a second time into his mother's womb to be born!"

Jesus answered, "I tell you the truth, unless a man is born of water and the Spirit, he cannot enter the kingdom of God (John 3:1-5).

When you receive Christ by personal invitation, He comes to live in you. Jesus said, *Here I am! I stand at the door and knock. If anyone hears my voice and opens the door, I will come in and eat with him, and he with me* (Revelation 3:20).

Receiving Christ means turning to God from self

and changing your mind about your sinful life (repentance) and trusting Christ to come into your life to forgive your sins and to make you the kind of person He wants you to be. Just to agree intellectually that Jesus Christ is the Son of God and that He died on the cross for your sins is not enough. Nor is it enough to have an emotional experience. You receive Jesus Christ by faith, as an act of the will.

You can receive Christ right now by faith through prayer. God knows your heart and is not so concerned with your words as He is with the attitude of your heart.

Here is a suggested prayer:

"Lord Jesus, I need You. I admit my life has been going the wrong direction. I know that I could never be good enough to be forgiven for my sins. Thank You for dying on the cross so I could have forgiveness and eternal life. I want You to make me the kind of person You want me to be. Amen."

Does this prayer express the desire of your heart? If it does, pray it now and Christ will come into your life as He promised.

The Bible promises eternal life to all who receive Christ: *And this is the testimony: God has given us eternal life, and this life is in his Son. He who has the Son has life; he who does not have the Son of God does not have life. I write these things to you who believe in the name of the Son of God so that you may know that you have eternal life* (1 John 5:11-13).

Continue to grow

After you have committed your life to Christ, continue to grow in Him. You have been born again, but do not stay as a baby in Christ. Continue to grow spiritually, to become strong and mature in your Christian walk. How? Let me suggest these ways:

1. Yield your life to Jesus Christ daily.

2. Obey Christ daily. You must deny yourself to obey God and His Word.

3. Pray daily. Devote time every day to talk with God in prayer. He is your new heavenly Father. Talk to Him as you would to your earthly father. Tell Him your troubles, ask Him for advice, tell Him you love Him, and thank Him for all He has done in your life. We don't have to make an appointment because we know that we have the King of kings and Lord of lords available to us 24 hours a day. He is there in times of trouble, sickness, or joy to guide and comfort us. Prayer is the intimate conversation between you and your heavenly Father.

4. Spiritual growth. Read your Bible daily. This is the food you need to mature spiritually. This is the only guidebook God has given us. Study it with the help and inspiration of the Holy Spirit by faith—not by your personal feelings.

It is impossible to earn a diploma in high school or college by going to class only one hour a week and never doing your homework. Nor can you understand the Bible unless you study it. Your mind and spirit will be developed by what you read and study in God's Word.

5. Worship. Do you attend church in the same way you attend a movie or play? You enjoy what you hear but it doesn't really affect your life? When your pastor preaches the Word, ask the Holy Spirit to apply it to your life. Practice what you've heard preached.

Most of us are willing to spend four to five hours a week playing a sport, watching a movie, or doing something else we enjoy, but few of us spend four to five hours a week in prayer, Bible study, and worship. The things of this world will some day fade away. They are only temporal. But the things of God are for eternity.

6. Witness. If you were to meet the President of the United States face-to-face and have a personal talk with him, you couldn't wait to tell everyone of your experience. Yet, the President is only a man. As a Christian, you walk and talk with the Creator of the universe, God Almighty. Isn't He much greater? Are you telling the people around you about Him?

Jesus said, *"If anyone is ashamed of me and my words in this adulterous and sinful generation, the Son of Man will be ashamed of him when he comes in his Father's glory with the holy angels"* (Mark 8:38). He also promised us power: *"You will receive power when the Holy Spirit comes on you; and you will be my witnesses in Jerusalem, and in all Judea and Samaria, and to the ends of the earth"* (Acts 1:8).

Don't let any opportunities go by without telling others about your Savior and what He has done and is doing for you. Let them know who is Number One in your life. What a glorious opportunity to share the life-changing power of Jesus Christ with a neighbor or friend! The greatest day of your life was when you accepted Jesus as Lord and Savior. And the second greatest day could only be when you led a loved one, friend, or even a stranger to a personal relationship with Jesus Christ. Proverbs 11:30 says, *He who wins souls is wise.*

7. Praise daily. Every day, praise God for who He is and what He has done in your life.

8. Conversion. True conversion involves the total mind, affection, and will. An intellectual experience is not enough. Many believe in the Bible, God,

67

and Jesus, but they have never been converted. Conversion means you have a change in the way you live, in your attitudes and priorities and in the things you hate (sin) and love (truth). You have power over the things of this world. If these changes haven't begun in your life, you have every right to doubt your salvation.

9. Tithe. After eating in a restaurant, most of us don't think anything at all about leaving a 10- or 15 percent tip for the waitress. But how many of us are willing to give that much of our earnings to the Lord? A ten dollar bill looks so big in the offering plate at church but so little when we spend it at the grocery store.

Never try to save your material goods from God. He deserves everything you are and own. Giving to God is no loss; it is putting your money in the best bank in the universe where it draws the greatest interest. Jesus said, *"Do not store up for yourselves treasures on earth, where moth and rust destroy, and where thieves break in and steal. But store up for yourselves treasures in heaven, where moth and rust do not destroy, and where thieves do not break in and steal. For where your treasure is, there your heart will be also* (Matthew 6:19-21).

Giving is true having. As one old gravestone said of the man's whose grave it marked: "What I spent I had, what I saved I lost, what I gave I have."

10. Serve. Commit *yourself* to God's work by giving of your time and talent. Serve as an usher, sing in the choir, volunteer in the church office. There IS something you can do. Serve!

I have three sons, and my daily prayer is that they will grow spiritually and experience the abundant life God has to offer. I pray that they and their families will commit themselves to doing the ten things I have listed in this chapter.

My youngest son, Ron, memorized "The Four Spiritual Laws" when he was eight years old. From this, he has gradually built a solid Christian foundation in his life. Today, he is serving God, and is on the board of a well-known Christian evangelist.

I trust that every person who is reading this book will consider commiting his or her life to Jesus and will continue to grow spiritually until we meet in heaven. I pray that, just as you obey the physical laws of the universe, you will also come to understand and obey the spiritual laws of God so that you will find eternal, abundant life.

Practicing the ten basic principles listed in this chapter will help you learn to live a spiritual life. How do you think you're doing in these areas now? Take a moment to rate yourself. Honestly evaluate your performance on each item on a scale of 1 to 10. Then add up your total to get an idea of your personal spiritual relationship with God.

1._____   5._____   9._____

2._____   6._____   10._____

3._____   7._____   Total_____

4._____   8._____

Are you satisfied? If not, work toward spiritual growth by concentrating on the areas where you scored lowest. Don't put it off. Do it now while there is still time.

Chapter 7

The Big Bang

In the October/November 1988 issue of *Modern Maturity* magazine (published by the American Association of Retired People (AARP) was an article by J. I. Merritt entitled, "The Birth of Everything." The article was about the "Big Bang Theory," which holds that the universe began with a huge explosion from which the universe and everything in it eventually evolved. This theory says that out of chaos came harmony and all the laws of nature.

Throughout his discussion of this theory, Mr. Merritt uses the following words and phrases:

If...

Perhaps...

Scenario...

We think...

New findings will require us to go back to the drawing board...

Two "Big Bang" scientists with theories that contradict each other...

Theories that continue to change...

Hypothetical...

In his last paragraph, Mr. Merritt quotes James

Peebles, a leading astronomer and cosmologist at Princeton University. Mr. Peebles likens the "Big Bang" scientists who are attempting to comprehend the universe to slightly befuddled kindergarten children. The "children" are patiently taught by Nature who, says Mr. Merritt, "keeps presenting us with hints. We're still not getting the point, but at last we're working toward it."

God created the universe

Does all of this sound confusing to you? I'll never understand how intelligent people can believe that our universe somehow just happened, that all the laws of nature and the order in the universe somehow, someway just evolved from chaos. It takes more faith to believe that nonsense than it does to believe the truth—that God created the universe.

Many people believe the "Big Bang" theory because it allows them to NOT believe in God. They don't have to recognize God (and therefore believe His Word) if they can prove everything just happened by itself.

Mr. Merritt evidently feels the Bible holds no more truth than other "creation myths." He says, "From Genesis to the creation myths of aboriginal tribes, human beings have always sought answers to the cosmic question: How did the universe begin?" He continues, "Only in the last 60 years have astronomers and physicists acquired the information to piece together a scientific picture of how the universe was born and evolved, and how it might end."

I know how the universe began because the Bible, written thousands of years ago, tells me how it began. Mr. Merritt implies that only science can give us the real picture of how the universe was born and that the

Bible's picture is only a myth. How sad that people refuse to believe the truth when it is so clear and simple!

Merritt said, "As Stephen Hawking, perhaps the most brilliant theoretical physicist since Einstein, writes, the attempt to answer these questions is an attempt to understand the mind of God."

We don't have to "attempt" to understand the mind of God. The Bible very clearly tells us that God created the universe and why He made it. If these scientists want to find the truth about the universe, all they have to do is read God's Word. The Bible is the MIND of God. It may not answer all their questions or disprove all their theories, but it will give them the most critical answers they seek. God's Word proves that the beginning of creation didn't happen by chance but by the will and power of God.

Why believe a theory like the "Big Bang" which is constantly being changed, re-evaluated, questioned? Every time a new discovery takes place, scientists have to change their theories to fit the facts. I would much rather believe the Genesis account of creation which has been in existence for thousands of years without change. Thousands of scholars have tried unsuccessfully to find just one error in it.

As of now, all the evidence scientists have uncovered has simply confirmed that the universe is the work of an orderly, intelligent being—God. And I believe that all the evidence uncovered by scientists in the future will simply confirm over and over again that God is the Master and Maker of creation.

Men want to be their own gods

The reason men look for possibilities other than God for the creation of the universe and life is that they don't want to acknowledge God. Like Adam and Eve in the Garden, they want to be their own gods. They don't want to serve anyone other than themselves.

This is why the theory of evolution is so widely accepted even though it has very little proof to back it up. If people can disprove God, they can do away with the Ten Commandments and the moral laws God laid down in the Bible. If they can do away with God, they do away with sin and its consequences. Man becomes the measure for himself. He can do as he pleases because he decides what is right and wrong.

Unfortunately, while we try to convince ourselves that God doesn't exist, our lives prove over and over again that He does. The Bible says, *Do not be deceived: God cannot be mocked. A man reaps what he sows. The one who sows to please his sinful nature, from that nature will reap destruction; the one who sows to please the Spirit, from the Spirit will reap eternal life* (Galatians 6:7, 8).

The state of our nation and the world today proves this to be true. We are overcome with divorce, drug abuse, murder, greed, disease, homelessness, rape, alcoholism, etc. We struggle with what is right and what is wrong. We border on the brink of destroying ourselves with war, pollution, and disease. We are a world out of control. Yet, all this would change if we would acknowledge that God is sovereign, that His Word is true, and turn in true repentance back to Him.

Second Chronicles 7:14 says, *"If my people, who are called by my name, will humble themselves and pray and seek my face and turn from their wicked ways, then will I hear from heaven and will forgive their sin and will heal their land."*

Do you want to know where creation began? Read Genesis 1 and 2. Then make your choice. The Bible will tell you the plain simple facts, and those facts won't change with the passing of time. They are true for now and all eternity. Will you believe the "Big Bang" scientists who contradict each other, who constantly change their theories, and who have scant proof of what they say? Or will you believe God in His unchangeable, infallible Word?

Chapter 8

Creation

When I read the article mentioned in the last chapter, I was very disturbed. I feel that the "Big Bang Theory" is untrue and unproven. Yet, the American Association of Retired Persons (AARP) devoted eight pages of their monthly magazine, *Modern Maturity*, to promote it.

I wrote to the editor and urged her to give the biblical story of creation equal time in the magazine. Unfortunately, she refused. This, I feel, is a real disservice to the people who support the AARP and read its magazine.

Here is an organization that is doing much to help senior citizens by providing information about health, insurance, and other ways to improve their lives. Yet this same organization will not provide them information about life AFTER the grave. I can only think that the AARP is satisfied to let their constituents believe we are only here by chance and the grave is the end of us all.

In reality, the grave is the beginning of eternity. And we can and MUST prepare for it NOW, in this life. We each must make a choice to serve God and spend eternity with Him in heaven or choose to not serve God and spend eternity without Him in hell.

This information is more important than any theories about how the universe began or what may possibly happen to it billions of years in the future. This information can affect the lives of millions of people who are living right now and who will soon be facing eternity. Therefore, I would like to share my thoughts about creation and what the Bible says about it.

In the beginning God...

The Bible says, *In the beginning God created the heavens and the earth* (Genesis 1:1). Every scientist who studies creation with an open mind must finally admit that there had to be a creator and that creator was God. They may not accept the God of Judo-Christian belief, but they must accept that the universe was created by an intelligent supreme being.

In the Genesis account, the creation of the universe is described in detail:

✦ On the first day, God created the heavens and the earth, light and darkness. He called the light "day" and the darkness "night."

✦ On the second day, God separated the water covering the earth from the atmosphere and created the sky.

✦ On the third day, God separated the water from the land and created all the plants and trees.

✦ On the fourth day, God created the sun, moon, and all the planets of the universe.

✦ On the fifth day, God made all the creatures of the water and air.

✦ On the sixth day, God created all the land animals and, finally, man.
✦ On the seventh day, God finished His work and rested.

For years scientists have been trying to prove their theories of creation, including the "Big Bang Theory," without much success. They keep saying in only a few more years or with a few more discoveries, they will find the evidence they need to prove what they've been saying. But the years pass, they make more and more discoveries about the universe, and still they haven't proven their theories. In fact, if anything they keep proving over and over again that the universe couldn't have begun by itself, that only an intelligent, orderly being could have created it.

The universe did not happen by chance

There is such a wealth of evidence today disproving the "Big Bang Theory" that it isn't given much credence by those who are well informed. Despite this, students are still being taught that the complexity of the universe and of life came about merely by random chance. And when those of us who want the truth taught in public schools ask that Creationism be given equal time, we are called religious fanatics and Creationism is labeled a myth.

It is absurd to believe that the universe and life happened by chance. It is as absurd as believing a simple pocket watch could come into being by chance. Beneath its face are coils, wheels, and other intricate mechanisms, each one working precisely together with the others to measure and display the correct time.

Now, for a simple experiment. Suppose you smash that watch with a hammer. You give it a good BANG.

Then you shake all the pieces together for a few million years. Do you really think the parts will assemble themselves in the correct order and once again start measuring and displaying the time?

Of course not! Yet, this is basically what the "Big Bang Theory" would have us believe about something infinitely more complex than a simple watch—the universe. Scientists want us to believe that "At the moment of creation, all the matter that would one day form into galaxies, stars, planets and people was packed into a speck smaller than a virus," that the speck exploded and expanded and eventually became stars, that on one (or more) of those stars conditions were just right and some of the right molecules came together to create life, and that that life evolved in such a way to eventually become man.

Do you believe that's how the universe and life came to be? I doubt it! Just look at the DNA molecule, the building block of life. What are the chances that the DNA molecule, in all its complexities, could have just evolved?

Biochemists have discovered that the chemical configuration for just one rung of human DNA is 10 to the 87th power (10 followed by 87 zeros). They believe it would have taken far longer than the 4.5 billion years of earth's existence for that one rung of the DNA molecule to be created by chance. The incredibly complex design of DNA—and of life itself —points to a supreme designer, God.

Just as modern skyscrapers are evidence of careful planning by an intelligent creator, so, too, the universe is evidence of careful planning by an intelligent creator. The idea that our universe began with a big bang and evolved by chance makes as much sense as the idea that an explosion in a junk yard could produce a rocket ship.

Many scientists believe the Bible

There are many scientists today, with impressive credentials, who believe in the Bible's creation story. One of them, Dr. Russell Mixter, is a member and past president of the American Scientific Affiliation and author of *Creation and Evolution.*

Dr. Mixter states in his book that scripture declares that God the creator is all-knowing and all-powerful. He made living organisms to His own plan and purpose, and He made many organisms. Darwin, on the other hand, advocated total evolution. He believed that life began with only one organism which evolved into many others.

Even today, evolutionists are looking for the "missing link" that ties all life forms together. But they haven't found it yet, and I don't believe they ever will. Why? Because it never existed. Evolution cannot be proven because creation didn't happen that way. I suppose, however, that evolutionists will go on looking for their "missing link" and many people will go on accepting as fact what simply cannot be proven scientifically.

Genesis 1 uses the phrase "according to their various kinds" over and over again. It speaks of plants bearing seed according to their kinds, trees bearing fruit with seed in it according to their kinds, creatures of the sea according to their kinds, and birds according to their kinds, etc. This account cuts squarely across Darwin's theory. The "kinds" of Genesis did not evolve; they were specifically created by God.

The Bible does not conflict with science

When the Bible speaks on scientific matters and is correctly interpreted, it does not conflict with the findings of science. Notice, I said findings, not theories. The Bible DOES conflict with certain theories which CANNOT be proven. But true findings of science have never and will never contradict the truth of the Bible.

Please don't think I am anti-science because I'm not. Science can be a wonderful tool to help mankind or it can be a weapon to destroy him. Consider three examples:

✦ Knowledge of the atom can be used to create energy for man's use or to create weapons to destroy mankind.

✦ Knowledge of bacteria can be used to fight human disease or it can be used in bacteriological warfare to kill humans.

✦ Knowledge of the universe and life can be used in an attempt to prove that God does not exist, leaving mankind with no hope, or it can be used to show the greatness and majesty of God and bring man closer to God.

Dr. Irving W. Knobloch, a scientist listed in "Who's Who In America," has written many articles in scientific journals through the years. He states that science can and should deal only with the observable and the measurable. Instead, many scientists seem more concerned with promoting their theories instead of finding the truth.

Science, says Dr. Knobloch, is not omnipotent. It can't account for or explain everything. Science cannot, for example, prove or disprove the existence of

God. Religious beliefs such as the plan of redemption, the incarnation, and eternal life fall outside the realm of science.

Neither can science explain the origin of the universe. Scientists may speculate and offer theories but they do not have enough evidence to prove that the universe was created solely by chance. And, in order to believe that it was, they must have as much faith as a Christian does to believe that God created it.

I am a Christian by faith. I believe some things I do not understand and cannot explain because I believe in God—the authority of my life. Even if I do not understand certain things in His Word, if I obey Him, I know they will work because He said they would.

Science also must believe its authorities. But those authorities are always in question. Science must constantly check and recheck its authorities to see if they are true and have remained true through the passing of time. Scientists run into trouble, however, when they begin believing supposition instead of fact, when they believe what they have not proved, when they treat theory as proven fact.

There is nothing intrinsic in science that will lead a person into atheism. There isn't anything evil in proper scientific experiments and procedures. Examining something scientifically doesn't make one an atheist. The evil comes when the results of scientific research are used in the wrong way or for the wrong reasons. It is wrong for scientists to take the little we do know about the universe, for example, and try to twist it into proving something that we do not know.

The best scientists can say at this point is:

✦ Science cannot prove who or what created the universe.

✦ Science cannot prove conclusively how the universe was created.

✦ Science can show that the universe is well ordered and logical.

✦ Science can show that the universe was created and is still operating according to certain well-defined, constant laws.

Many scientists have been led to a faith in God by observing the wonders of the universe. But that is what it is—faith. Science cannot prove God. We must accept Him or reject Him on the basis of our own personal faith.

We must come to God in faith

I think all Christians doubt at one time or another, and there's nothing necessarily wrong with that. If we doubt, it means we're questioning and seeking to know the truth. After all, God simply hasn't told us everything. There's a lot He has kept hidden from us. Why? Because He wants us to come to Him in faith.

If God had told us everything in His Word (which He could have done) we wouldn't have to use our faith. We wouldn't have to trust Him and lean on Him to guide us and help us. We wouldn't need God, or at least we would think that we didn't.

God has given us all the information we need to make a decision for or against Him. *Without faith,* says Hebrews 11:6, *it is impossible to please God, because anyone who comes to him must believe* [that's faith] *that he exists and that he rewards those who earnestly seek him.*

Second Corinthians 5:7 says, *We live by faith, not by sight.* Galatians 3:11 tells us that, *"The righteous will live by faith."* And Ephesians 2:8 says, *It is by grace you have been saved, THROUGH FAITH.*

We must simply accept by faith many things which cannot be proved scientifically. I do not know, for example, all of the details of how God created the universe, but I know without a doubt that He created it according to Genesis 1. I do not know exactly what heaven will look like, but because God has said in His Word that He has prepared heaven for us, I know I will go there when I die.

The real test of a scientific experiment is whether or not it works. The real test of our Christian faith is whether or not it works. The greatest proof of Christianity to me is not what I have observed in my years of study, but it is the Christ-like life I have seen in other Christians and the indwelling of Christ at work in me.

There are thousands of things every day that we do not understand and yet we accept by faith. Whenever we plug a lamp into an outlet and turn on the switch, we have faith that the lamp will work and the light will come on. We can't see the electricity passing through the cord. We probably don't understand how it works. But we know it works because we have experienced it. We've learned that when we plug in a lamp and turn on the switch, the light will come on. And that's how much of Christianity is—we believe it because it works.

How we know the Bible is true

Art Crawford of Columbus, Ohio, worked with Einstein on the atomic bomb, inventing the detonator that triggered the weapon. He has several hundred scientific accomplishments to his credit and is well known in scientific circles.

Dr. Crawford has said that one way we can know the Bible is true is by looking at the prophecies about Jesus. These prophecies, recorded in the Old Testament, were all written at least 300 or more years before the birth of Christ. Yet, each and every one came true just before or during Jesus' lifetime. Many of the prophecies were about things and events over which Jesus had no control; yet, they all happened just as the Old Testament prophets said they would.

What are the chances of that happening by chance? Suppose you were to make a prophecy that tomorrow there would be an automobile accident. The mathematical probability of your being right is one chance in two. Now suppose you add to your prophecy. You say there is going to be an accident tomorrow and it is going to happen at 12:00 noon. What is the mathematical probability of your being right, now? Your chances of being right have gone up to one in four.

For every modification you make to your prophecy, the mathematical probability of your being correct doubles. If you say that the accident will be between a Chevrolet and a Buick; that one will be a 1981 model and the other a 1987 model; that one driver will be a woman and the other a man, your chances of being right are now one in 32.

If you were to add ten modifications to your original prophecy, the chances of this event taking place just as you prophesied would be one chance in two raised to the tenth power, that is, one chance in 2,048.

There are 333 prophecies in the Old Testament specifically concerning the birth and life of Jesus Christ. What is the mathematical probability of all 333 happening exactly as they were prophesied? It would be one chance in two raised to the 333rd power.

I don't know what that figure is, but I do know

that it is larger than the national debt. This number is so large that no one should ever doubt that Jesus Christ is exactly who the Bible says He is.

Christ's virgin birth was prophesied in Isaiah 7:14 and fulfilled in Matthew 1:18-23. The birth place was prophesied in Micah 5:2 and fulfilled in Luke 2:4-7. The reason for His death is foretold in Isaiah 53:4-6 and described in 1 Peter 2:24. The crucifixion described in Psalm 22 is related again in Matthew 27. The Resurrection prophesied in Psalm 16:9,10 was fulfilled according to Acts 2:31.

I'm told there are more than 300 of these fulfilled prophecies in the Bible. I would rather believe facts that have existed for several thousands of years and are still unchanged than the here-today-changed-to-morrow theories of some scientists. The Word of God is trustworthy and true; it will never change.

Who created life?

Scientists have made many advancements today. They can alter the DNA of one organism with the DNA of another. They can bring two cells together in a petri dish and help a new life begin. What they CANNOT do, however, is create life. We may alter, change, or destroy life but we cannot create it. Only God can do that.

There is very little in scientific literature today about life evolving by chance. This is for the very simple reason that scientists understand more clearly today the complexity of living things. With the invention of the electron miscrocope, scientists have been able to examine even the simplest of living things, and they have discovered how truly sophisticated and complex these creatures are. Most scientists today will readily grant that, however life happened, it did not—it COULD NOT—happen by chance.

A scientists can make an egg which looks like an egg, smells like an egg, and even tastes like an egg, but it won't hatch! The life in the egg can only come from God.

Atheists want desperately to believe that man evolved by chance because that would do away with God. Instead of God making man, man would have invented God. But they have no facts to back up their claims of evolution. For every fact that they say proves evolution, there are many others to disprove it.

The problem, you see, is not a scientific one but a moral one. The primary difference between evolution and creationism does not center on man's beginning as an ape or in the Garden of Eden. It centers on Calvary because there is no room for a redeemer in evolutionism.

If, as evolution claims, man is continually evolving upward, he does not need a redeemer. God and sin are only myths man invented to help him understand his universe, and as he evolves into a superior being, he will no longer need these myths. That is why a Christian can never accept evolutionism. It is contrary to what the Bible teaches.

The strongest creationism evidence is man himself. Unlike the animals, man can make intelligent choices. He has a conscience and can make moral decisions. He is capable of love and self-sacrifice. And he seeks a God to worship. These qualities were not formed by accident. God created man in His image, to be above the animals He had created. He created man with a soul and with free will. And because man disobeyed God (and is still disobeying Him), he needs a Redeemer to change him back into the perfect creation he once was.

Atheists say Christians have no proof of God's existence, but the proof is all around us. Romans 1:18-20 says, *The wrath of God is being revealed from heaven against all the godlessness and wickedness of men who suppress the truth by their wickedness, since what may be known about God is plain to them, because God has made it plain to them. For since the creation of the world God's invisible qualities—his eternal power and divine nature—have been clearly seen, being understood from what has been made, so that men are without excuse.*

In creation, God shows us His power and super intelligence. The unending size of the universe and its amazing physical laws and beauty reveal the God who created it. Man can only understand a small part of God's creation because we are limited, mortal beings trying to understand the mind of a limitless, immortal being.

God's Word is more proof of His existence. There are 66 books in the Bible, written over thousands of years, by many individuals. Yet, none of the books contradict any of the others. In fact, all of the books contain the same message—man's rebellion from God and God's great forgiveness and love. Such a book cannot be the work of mere mortals; it was inspired by God's Holy Spirit.

After 2,000 years, no expert has yet disproved a single statement in the Bible. The reason is, *All Scripture is God-breathed* (2 Timothy 3:16). It is not the work of men but of God.

God is eternal, just, perfect, all-knowing, all-present, all-powerful. The Bible reveals many truths about God, but it cannot disclose the full truth about

89

God because we wouldn't and couldn't understand it. If we could understand God completely, He would be unworthy of our worship.

Science is God

To the atheist, science is God and education is its power. But science has failed in its attempt to build a better world with education. The atheist says that if people could only be educated enough, then greed, killing, etc.—all of the many evils in our world—would end. If only we could understand our fellowman, then we would love each other.

The sad truth is, science and education have failed to give us a perfect world or to change the nature of man. Some of the most educated people in history have been the most corrupt. While science and education do make life better in some ways, they cannot solve man's moral problems.

I am not against education. But I strongly believe that God MUST be in our educational picture. *Knowledge puffs up, but love builds up* (1 Corinthians 8:1). We can teach people that they should love their neighbor, but we cannot make them or empower them to love their neighbor.

When man becomes educated sufficiently, he becomes puffed up, filled with pride. He no longer needs God. He feels he has sufficient wisdom to solve all his problems. He becomes his own god. Ultimately, however, he comes up against some problem, some event over which he has no power. When disease, disaster, or death strikes, he finds that his wisdom is not enough to save him.

In the 1940s, Germany was one of the most educated nations of the world, filled with universities and schools. German scholars and scientists were far ahead of others in the world. They created plastics and synthetics before any other country. They had guided missiles and the latest of every sort of electronic and mechanical device.

Yet, these educated people put a madman into power. When Hilter ruled Germany, he took all the good that country's scholars and scientists had discovered and turned it into something evil and destructive. This nation of educated people wrote a page of history that was filled with killing and persecution unlike any the modern world had seen. All their science and education could not and did not make them better or more moral people.

Our gadgets cannot save us

Science has failed to build a better world with gadgets. Our automobiles, super planes, radio, television, refrigerators, VCRs, etc., have failed to make us better people or our world a better place. Our lives are so full of gadgets that life has become easier in many ways, but WE have not become better.

Our electronic industry has succeeded in inventing equipment that can do everything except think. Our machinery is more productive and more reliable in many ways than the people who run them. Yet, our machinery has not made us better people. We are taking all this sophisticated knowledge and developing more accurate and deadly weapons. All our gadgetry may bring us temporary happiness. It may make our lives easier and fuller. But it cannot make us better people or go with us beyond the grave.

We like to think that we are in control of our own destinies, that mankind rules the world, but the truth is, God is still in control of this world. Romans 13:1 says, *There is no authority except that which God has established. The authorities that exist have been established by God.*

The Prophet Daniel wrote, *"Praise be to the name of God for ever and ever; wisdom and power are his. He changes times and seasons; he sets up kings and deposes them. He gives wisdom to the wise and knowledge to the discerning. He reveals deep and hidden things; he knows what lies in darkness, and light dwells with him"* (Daniel 2:20-22).

Historians say that the race to build the atom bomb in World War II was barely won by the Allies; Germany could easily have won except for a few events. But I don't believe that. The reason the United States built the atom bomb first was because God intervened and allowed us to build it. If Germany had won World War II, much of the world today would probably be enslaved. But God did not allow that to happen. One of the mightiest displays of His grace to our nation was in His allowing us to win that war.

How ironic that God not only allowed us to build the atom bomb first, but He used many German people to do it. Many scientists fled Germany when they saw how evil Hilter was. If they had stayed, Germany might have built the bomb first. But God did not allow that to happen. And when the war was over, He used these same German scientists who had come to this country to help lead us into our great space program.

Science cannot save mankind. Education cannot save mankind. Medicine cannot save us. Only the liberating, redeeming power of God can save us. Through His Son, Jesus Christ, He has shown us how we are to love our neighbor, and through His Holy Spirit, He empowers us to do so.

Atheists are blind

No atheist who has studied the facts, can truthfully deny God, Christ, and the Bible. If he did, he would have to accept the truth of God's existence. An atheist who doesn't believe in God is simply blinding himself to the bankruptcy of his philosophy. He continues through life, avoiding reality and believing in the unbelieveable—the goodness of man.

I'm reminded of the story about a blind man walking through London's Hyde Park one morning. He heard an atheist denying the existence of God, declaring that he had never seen God, never spoke to Him, never heard Him speak. Therefore, he concluded, God was a fraud and only fools could believe in Him.

After the atheist stepped off the speaker's box, the blind man asked someone to help him get up on the box to speak.

The blind man told how, as he entered Hyde Park, he could smell the roses and the fresh grass, he could feel the sun warming his body and the wind against his cheek. But he had never seen them because he was blind. He went on to say, "As surely as there are roses, grass, sunshine and wind—there is a God who is everywhere. But the man who spoke before me is blind."

Since my death, I realize that there is a difference between feelings and facts. Feelings are different in each and every person. They vary according to the situation. But facts are established by proving what is true. They never vary. Facts are the same for every person.

What kind of doctor, lawyer, or professional person would you be if you only spent a short time studying for your profession? You must put in many years of searching, studying, and practice before you know the facts and are successful in your profession. Even a lifetime of study isn't enough to know all there is to know.

Yet, an atheist dismisses all the evidence and says God doesn't exist. He passes judgment on something he hasn't studied adequately and doesn't understand. He makes claims that he cannot substantiate with facts. He puts his trust and faith in his own intellect. Unfortunately, he will someday face eternity, and then he will have to face the truth. Only then will it be too late.

Science and education have failed us. The Bible says, *Love never fails...where there is knowledge, it will pass away* (1 Corinthians 13:8). Put your faith in God and His Word today. He will never fail you!

Chapter 9

We Are All Born Equal

One of the greatest topics of discussion today is, when does life begin? When does the human embryo become a person?

I believe life begins when the father's sperm attaches to the mother's egg. Within hours, the one single cell resulting from that union has split into other cells and a new life is beginning. Every genetic detail of a new person is there—the color of the skin, eyes, and hair; the shape of the face; the basic personality traits; the height and structure of the body. All are firmly established in that tiny embryo.

One cell becomes two, two becomes four, four becomes eight. The process continues until a tiny body forms and attaches itself to the inside of its mother's womb. After two weeks, the embryo is only one-tenth of an inch long, but already the body is forming.

By the 24th day, all the bones and organs are in place. The heart has begun to beat. The arms and legs are visible. All the muscles and nerves are present, and the embryo begins to move. It is now one-fourth of an inch long—40 times larger than the original cell.

Medical science has observed, verified, and reported all these miraculous events to us.

Medicine has made great advances in the past 20 years. In fact, doctors can take an egg from a woman and a sperm from a man, put them together in a petri dish and start the process of life. Then they can put the fertilized egg back into a woman's body to develop, and the resulting child we call a "test tube baby." But who really created that life—man or God?

We may help the processes of life along, but we cannot create life. We may put the egg and the sperm together, but we cannot put the spark of life in the resulting cell. Nor can we guarantee that a child will develop from that cell. Only God can do that.

God created you

Your life began as soon as your mother's egg was fertilized by your father's sperm. Within that tiny cell was the blueprint for the person you would become. All your distinct features were there. And God oversaw the creative process that resulted in that tiny cell one day becoming a living, breathing baby—YOU!

You were molded by God. Even before you were born, He knew you. The psalmist wrote, *You* [God] *created my inmost being; you knit me together in my mother's womb. I praise you because I am fearfully and wonderfully made; your works are wonderful, I know that full well. My frame was not hidden from you when I was made in the secret place. When I was woven together in the depths of the earth, your eyes saw my unformed body. All the days ordained for me were written in your book before one of them came to be* (Psalm 139:13-16).

We are all equal to God

God made you. He gave you talents and abilities that make you unique and wonderful. He made each of us to be what we are. We are all equal in God's sight—no one is better than another.

According to the world's standard, however, people are not created equal. Some are more beautiful, more talented, more intelligent, more athletically gifted than others, and the world rewards them more because of it. But to God we are all created equal. He loves us each the same and gives us the gifts and talents He wants us to have. All He asks is that we use them the best we can.

Jesus told a parable in Matthew 25:14-30 about a man who was going away on a journey. Before he left, he gave his servants gifts. To one he gave five talents, to another two, and to another, one. When the man returned, he awarded each of his servants according to how well they had used the talents he had given them.

This story shows that God has given some of us more abilities than He has given others, but each of us has some God-given talent. It also shows that God expects us to use the gifts He has given us. If you develop yours and use them, God will reward you with more. But if you let your abilities lie dormant and never use them, you will lose them. Your life and your potential will have been wasted.

Determination is more important than abilities

God wants us to strive to be the very best we can be. He wants us to use our gifts to the fullest extent possible. That takes determination and hard work. It means never giving up. It means being a winner. And history has shown over and over again that it isn't so much the abilities (or disabilities) you are born with that make you a winner as it is your determination to succeed. When a person strives to be the best, nothing can hold him back. He will succeed.

The Jewish people are a good example of this. Down through history, I don't think any group has suffered more persecution than the Jews. They were in bondage in Egypt for hundreds of years. They were captives in Babylonia for many years. Their country was occupied by other nations off and on for centuries. During Jesus' time, they lost their nation and were scattered throughout the world. It has only been since 1948 that they have had their own nation again.

Yet, in spite of this, the Jews as a people have managed to not only survive but to prosper. In whatever country they have been, they have retained their identity, their culture, their religion, and their values. They have become successful in business, science, and entertainment, and they have held important positions of power in the nations in which they lived.

I believe this is because the Jews' religious and cultural heritage are rooted in their belief and worship of the one true God. God revealed himself to the Jews. He made a covenant with them and they became His people. Jews feel special. They have purpose. They have an identity that causes them to use their talents and abilities in the best way possible. Jews believe they are winners, and their lives reflect that belief. They are determined to do and be the best they can.

You are only as great as you strive to be. Look at the lives of Sammy Davis, Jr., Babe Ruth, Billy Graham, Helen Keller, Henry Ford, Oprah Winfrey, Bill Cosby, and others. These people rose above their circumstances to become successful as individuals. But they didn't make it by the color of their skin— white or black. They made it by developing their God-given talents through hard work, determination, and self-sacrifice. They have proved that, if you are willing to work hard and strive to be the best, you CAN be.

The most successful people in the world are those who have become all they can be in this life and prepared themselves for the next life. Look around you. The winners you see may include a grocery clerk, a company president, a housewife, a janitor, a nurse—anyone who lives his or her life with eternity in mind.

We are all equal in God's sight. He loves us each one the same, but it is OUR decision as to how successful we will be. God gives us each abilities, but it is up to US how well we use those abilities. Truly, we are born equal, but sadly enough, we don't all die that way.

God provides us the opportunities to receive salvation, the Holy Spirit, abundant living, immortality— and more, but it is up to us whether or not we seize these opportunities. Take a minute to think of all the things God has given you. Are you using them in the best ways you can? Are you using them to glorify God? Do you have a divine purpose for your life? Do you feel called, like a special child of God, a winner? You can!

Chapter 10

Death

Can you praise God when a loved one dies?

One Friday afternoon several years ago, the phone rang in Jacque Bourdeau's home. When he answered it, he was told his daughter had just been killed in an automobile accident.

Yvette was in her first year at Wheaton College in Chicago. She had been on her way home with two friends when the young man driving lost control of the car and it crashed. They were only a few miles from home.

Jacque has been a dear friend of mine for many years. We have worked together on Christian boards and in business. When I heard the tragic news of Yvette's death, I couldn't imagine how Jacque and his wife could bear losing a sweet daughter in the prime of her life.

My wife and I went to the funeral home, and among the many people there, I did not see a dry eye anywhere. I made my way over to Jacque, and he threw his arms around me. He was sobbing, tears streaming down his face. But he kept repeating, "Praise the Lord! Praise the Lord!"

Only a Christian can really understand how a person can praise God in the midst of grieving for a loved one. Jacque was crying his heart out. He loved his daughter and knew he would miss her terribly. But he also knew that Yvette loved the Lord and because she was now absent from the body, she was present with the Lord. He had the blessed assurance that someday he would spend eternity with Yvette in heaven. He was filled with the peace that only God can give.

An atheist cannot look past the grave, but Jacque could see past the grave into eternity...and rejoice. Could you?

Death is different for a Christian

Another friend of mine, Dave Penner, had a heart attack at his front door just a few days after my cardiac death. He died. He was a very respected doctor at Beaumont Hospital in Royal Oak, Michigan, and a born-again Christian for many years.

After his death, Dave's dear wife, Ruth, wrote me a sweet letter, praising the Lord for saving me and remarking that her beloved Dave had been promoted. Her heart was broken, but she also had that blessed assurance that only God can give that she will see and be with her husband again for all eternity.

What a difference a loved one's death can be when that one is a Christian. Philippians 1:21 says, *For to me, to live is Christ and to die is gain.* That's the Christian's attitude: to die is to be with the Lord for eternity. Jesus said, *"Come to me, all you who are weary and burdened, and I will give you rest. Take my yoke upon you and learn from me, for I am gentle and humble in heart, and you will find rest for your*

102

souls. *For my yoke is easy and my burden is light"* (Matthew 11:28-30).

Jesus died on a cross. He was tortured. A crown of thorns was pushed onto His head. He was whipped and beaten. He was spat upon and finally nailed to a cross. Even more dreadful than all of that, He was made to bear the sins of the world—your sins and mine—and finally, He died. He was buried in a borrowed grave, and after three days, God raised Him from the dead.

Why did Jesus go through all this suffering and death? So that you and I could be free from sin and receive eternal life. Hebrews 2:14,15 says about Jesus, *Since the children have flesh and blood, he* [Jesus] *too shared in their humanity so that by his death he might destroy him who holds the power of death—that is, the devil—and free those who all their lives were held in slavery by their fear of death.*

Because Jesus died and rose again, you and I don't have to fear death anymore. When we die as Christians, we are promoted to life everlasting with Jesus Christ.

After my experience with death, I reviewed my past life. I recognized all my sins and faults and I repented. Now I am striving to do what God wants me to do, totally, unreservedly. I wish I could say that I will never sin again. Oh, how I wish I could put the world, the flesh, and the devil behind me for the rest of my life. But none of us are perfect. Still, we have the assurance that, *If we confess our sins, he* [God] *is faithful and just and will forgive us our sins and purify us from all unrighteousness* (1 John 1:9). And as we strive to live for the Lord, as we obey Him, we become more and more like Him.

Now is the day of salvation

Our late President, John Kennedy, was one of the most powerful men in the world at the time of his death. He was wealthier than most, good looking, and talented. But the very second that a bullet ended his life, the only thing that mattered was his relationship with Christ. He couldn't take any of his worldly possessions with him. All his money and power couldn't change his eternal destination. The only thing that counted was whether or not he had accepted the free gift of salvation.

Ephesians 2:8,9 says, *For it is by grace you have been saved, through faith—and this not from yourselves, it is the gift of God—not by works, so that no one can boast.* God saves us through faith in Him, and our money, power, or talents don't really matter.

As a Christian, when I died I couldn't lose either way. Like the Apostle Paul said in Philippians 1:21, if I lived it was for God's glory and if I died I would be in heaven with Him. It was a win-win situation. But it wasn't because of any good I'd done. It was only because I had accepted Jesus Christ years ago and was born again.

None of us knows when death will come for us, but we all know death will surely come. Why take a chance? Death can come at any time, at any age, in any place. Not a day goes by but that thousands are swept into eternity with no warning.

When I share these truths with others, sometimes a person will say, "Oh, Bill, you're just trying to scare me."

"Yes, I am," I reply. "Eternity in hell is a scary thing. Hell is a place of torment that never ends. And if you die without accepting Jesus Christ as your Lord and Savior, hell will be your destination. I don't want

104

that to happen. Consider the facts, and then make a decision for Christ."

Too many of us are guided only by our feelings. "I don't feel like thinking about death right now..." or "I don't feel like accepting Jesus today..." or "I feel like I'm going to live forever." Don't let your feelings be your only motivation. Consider the facts and act on them.

Your life is like a train. The engine is the facts—God's facts, what His Word says. The engine should be fired by faith through the Holy Spirit. At the end of the train is the caboose, which is your feelings. You need the caboose but it doesn't pull the train.

Conversion is only the beginning

When you accept Jesus Christ and are born again, that is known as conversion. It is only the beginning. Conversion is the experience of moving from darkness to light, from death to life. It only happens once to each of us. Dedication, however, is an ongoing process. It starts at conversion and continues until death. Every day we rededicate our lives to Christ and, by doing so, we are transformed into His image. We become like Him.

The Apostle Paul told the Christians in Philippi to *continue to work out your salvation with fear and trembling, for it is God who works in you to will and to act according to his good purpose* (Philippians 2:12,13).

I think it is so sad that people become Christians and then remain spiritual babies. They never receive the joy of spiritual growth but remain in a carnal state. How do you grow? As I've discussed in previous chapters, you must:

105

✦ Study God's Word on a daily basis.
✦ Communicate with God each day through prayer.
✦ Witness to others of God's love and share His Word.
✦ Let God control every facet of your life through obedience to Him.

That's how you become a mature Christian. Paul described it this way: *Do your best to present yourself to God as one approved, a workman who does not need to be ashamed and who correctly handles the word of truth* (2 Timothy 2:15).

I am not afraid to die

Many people have asked me what it was like to be dead. What did I see? What did I do? The truth is, I don't remember. I don't know where I went or what I did. But I do know that I am not afraid to die. My fear of death is gone.

My mother, who was a Christian, wasn't afraid to die. I was with her the day before she passed away, and she was laughing and so happy. She wanted to tell me goodbye, and I knew she would miss me. But her desire was to be with the Lord. My dad and many of her loved ones were already in heaven, and Mother couldn't wait for that grand reunion she knew was waiting for her there.

Now that I've had one experience with death, I know I can die again any time, any place. I've come to understand how temporal life is. The psalmist wrote, *As for man, his days are like grass, he flourishes like a flower of the field; the wind blows over it and it is gone, and its place remembers it no more. But from everlasting to everlasting the Lord's love is with those who fear him* (Psalm 103:15-17).

God wants us to understand how transient life is. *Plan your life as if you had forever and live as if you only had today.*

In just the next 50 years, more than half of all the people on earth will be in eternity. Whether we like it or not, we must recognize that death can come to us or our loved ones at any moment, and we must adjust our lives to this fact. *Nothing is more certain than the fact of death, and nothing is more uncertain than the time of death.*

Death stalks the rich and poor, the educated and uneducated, the young and the old. He is no respecter of race, sex, age, or creed. The fear of him haunts us day by day, and we never know when that dreaded moment will come. So we take out insurance to cushion the blow. We exercise and eat right to hold off the inevitable. We invent devices to make our last days comfortable. We eat, drink, and are merry in an effort to forget. But the stark reality of death is always there.

The human part of us hates death. We will do anything to postpone it for a few days or hours. But wouldn't the world be a terrible place without the release of death? The crippled would be trapped in their crippled bodies forever. The blind would never see. The terminally ill would never cease to suffer.

All of us would like another chance at life. No matter how carefully we have lived, there are always things we would like to go back and do over. There are always mistakes we would like to correct. Wouldn't it be wonderful to die and start over again? Well, you can't ever go back and relive your life, but you can have another chance at living. As a Christian, you have the opportunity to live AFTER death.

Death breaks down the barriers of time and space. When we die, like Stanton said of Abraham Lincoln, we **"belong to the ages."** We had nothing to do with our coming into this world and we have little to do with our leaving it.

God has a place prepared for His children

When we were born, most of us had a place prepared for us. Our loving parents and friends provided all we needed to live. As Christians we can expect that same love and care from our heavenly Father. When, by death, we enter that other world, we will also have a place prepared for us. God will provide all we need to live forever. There will be no sorrow, pain, death, or sin.

Jesus said, *"Do not let your hearts be troubled. Trust in God; trust also in me. In my Father's house are many rooms; if it were not so, I would have told you. I am going there to prepare a place for you. And if I go and prepare a place for you, I will come back and take you to be with me that you also may be where I am"* (John 14:1-3).

Heaven is our eternal home. Our Lord is there and all Christians who have already died are also there. The Bible says, *"No eye has seen, no ear has heard, no mind has conceived what God has prepared for those who love him"* (1 Corinthians 2:9). So we can receive comfort in knowing that the passing of a Christian from this world is not a departure into the unknown but a move to a place prepared for him or her by the Lord Jesus. He died and rose from the dead, and He gives us the assurance that there is life after death—joyful, eternal life with Him.

Some people believe that death is the end of human existence. That simply isn't true. God's Word shows us that not only does death not end our existence, it does not even interrupt our existence. After death we continue to live. First Thessalonians 5:10 says, [Jesus] *died for us so that, whether we are awake* [alive] *or asleep* [dead], *we may live together with him.* As Christians, when we depart from this world we are still living with Christ. Though the body may be lying in the grave, the man himself, the tenant of the body, still lives on.

Death is like walking out of one room into another. Your body is only a temporal home. One day you shall move out of it, but you will continue to live. Your body will turn to dust but you will be eternally alive.

When John Quincy Adams was 80 years old, he met an old friend one day on the streets of Boston. The friend shook his trembling hand and said, "Good morning. How is John Adams today?"

"He is quite well, sir," replied the former President, "but the house in which he lives at present is becoming dilapidated. Time and the seasons have nearly destroyed it. Its roof is pretty well worn out. Its walls are much shattered, and it trembles with every wind. The old tenement is becoming almost uninhabitable, and I think John Adams will have to move out of it soon. But he himself is quite well, sir, quite well!"

That is the splendid testimony of a man who understood that the body will die, but the man within

109

lives on. In death, the man simply moves out of the body and into eternity.

What is death for a Christian? It is only a night's sleep when weariness and faintness pass away. Then the Spirit brings a new morning, and we arise, fresh and strong and joyous, alive for eternity.

For an atheist, the grave is the end. There is no morning; there is only night. If you fear the loss of health, growing old, death, remember: *God so loved the world that he gave his one and only Son, that whoever believes in him shall not perish but have EVERLASTING LIFE* (John 3:16).

No Christian has any reason to fear death any longer. We have victory over death through Jesus Christ. The Apostle Paul wrote, *"Where, O death, is your victory? Where, O death, is your sting? .... Thanks be to God! He gives us the victory through our Lord Jesus Christ"* (1 Corinthians 15:55, 57).

Chapter 11

The Solution to Sin

Although some people don't like to admit it, there is such a thing as sin. We are all sinners, incapable of changing ourselves. Romans 3:10-12 says, *There is no one righteous, not even one; there is no one who understands, no one who seeks God. All have turned away, they have together become worthless; there is no one who does good, not even one.*

No one can ever make himself right in God's sight by simply following rules and regulations. You can't earn your way into heaven. You can't do enough good deeds to outweigh the sin you have committed. Romans 3:20 says, *No one will be declared righteous in his [God's] sight by observing the law; rather, through the law we become conscious of sin.*

So how do we save ourselves? The truth is: we can't. Only God can save us. *A righteousness from God, apart from law, has been made known, to which the Law and the Prophets testify. This righteousness from God comes through faith in Jesus Christ to all who believe. There is no difference, for all have sinned and fall short of the glory of God, and are justified freely by his grace through the redemption that came by Christ Jesus* (Romans 3:21-24).

God has shown us that the way to heaven is not by being good or trying to keep His laws. God says He will accept us and acquit us of our sin only when we trust Jesus Christ to take away our sins. There is nothing we can do to save ourselves except to throw ourselves on God's mercy and believe that He will forgive us. When we do, we can all be saved by coming to Christ, no matter who we are or what we have done.

Do we have anything to boast about, then, when it comes to our salvation? Nothing at all. Our acquittal is not based on our good deeds but on what Christ has done and our faith in Him. We are saved by faith in Christ and not by the good things we do. *Jesus paid a debt he didn't owe because we had a debt we couldn't pay.*

If we are saved by faith, does this mean we no longer have to obey God's laws? No, just the opposite. Now we can obey God's laws because His Spirit lives in us and empowers us to obey.

Our minds are like computers. They have to be programmed. We can only get out of our minds what we put into them. If we fill our minds with good, we will think good thoughts. If we fill our minds with evil, our thoughts will be evil.

In our society, we flood our minds with pornography, liberalism, things against God, evil, filthy talk, dirty sex. We've outlawed the Bible in our schools. Over the past decade our moral standards have steadily gone downhill until cursing, adultery, unbelief, homosexuality, abortion, murder, etc., have become commonplace and acceptable. I am not just talking about

112

people without God but also about Christians who claim to believe in God.

How many Christian friends do you know who will watch an R-rated or X-rated movie and tell you how good it was? These are shows that use the Lord's name in vain, which depict murder, violence, rape, adultery, dishonesty, lying, and people jumping in and out of bed with each. Are you entertained by this? Remember, you only get out of your mind what you put in it.

Wouldn't you be a different person if you read the Bible daily? As you bathed your mind in God's Word and filled it with His promises, think how differently you would begin to think and act.

Who are you going to let program your mind, God or the devil? The choice is up to you. If you let the devil own your mind, the result will be death. Romans 6:23 says, *The wages of sin is death.* But if you let God own your mind, you will have eternal life through Jesus Christ. Psalm 51 promises that if you come to God, He will wash away all your iniquity and cleanse you from your sins. He will forgive you and make you whiter than snow.

Christians are not exempt

Sin, pornography, homosexuality, and sex dominate our movies, television, and other media. Moral standards have all but disappeared. Censorship is now considered gauche and unsophisticated. Phone companies and utility commissions have allowed dial-a-porn, obscenity, and sexually-oriented materials to invade telephones and televisions. Now you can dial a number and hear all sorts of filth and perversion—and YOU pay for it!

At a leading religious convention, attended by

many pastors and religious leaders, the management of the hosting hotel reported that 75 percent of the rooms occupied by "Bible-believing pastors" turned on X-rated movies. No other group who had used the hotel—lawyers, politicians, educators, etc.—had used the pay-for-sex channels as much as these pastors.

Sexual temptation is not limited to the world. Studies have shown that over 70 percent of born-again Christians have had sex outside of marriage. Sin is creeping into the minds and hearts of many good people, including Bible-believing Christians. Their minds are being filled, every day, with the immorality and garbage around us. And the more we ignore its presence, the uglier it grows.

People say, "Oh, a little bit of this and a little bit of that isn't going to hurt me. I'm a strong Christian."

The truth is, if you flirt with sin, it will end up destroying you. Like the old saying, you can't lay down with the pigs without getting up dirty. Sin is addictive. Little sins grow into big sins that will consume you and destroy your life.

Jesus said, *"The eye is the lamp of the body. If your eyes are good, your whole body will be full of light. But if your eyes are bad, your whole body will be full of darkness. If then the light within you is darkness, how great is that darkness! No one can serve two masters. Either he will hate the one and love the other, or he will be devoted to the one and despise the other"* (Matthew 6:22-24).

Sin is destroying our churches, ministers, and leaders. Events in recent years have seen the destruction of several powerful, national ministries and ministry leaders because of sin.

I know of one man who was working in one of the largest Christian ministries around. When he was caught practicing homosexuality, he was dismissed from that ministry, but he simply went to work for another. In time, he was found out by that ministry and fired. He simply went to work for another ministry and is still there today. How does he get away with this? Because he knows all the right words and actions to pass himself off as a Christian.

People like this man are just like Judas, one of Jesus' disciples. He traveled and lived with the other 11 disciples. He acted like them and looked just like them. When Jesus announced that one of the disciples was going to betray Him, they all looked at each other in disbelief. They couldn't imagine who the traitor might be. But Judas was a traitor, "the son of perdition" Jesus called him (see John 17:12, KJV). His life was full of sin, and it destroyed him.

Sin starts small and grows big

Judas didn't start out as a traitor. Somewhere along the line, he allowed sin into his life. That's always the way it begins. It starts with a thought, a suggestion. If we allow that thought to stay in our minds, it grows into a desire. And the desire, if it isn't quenched, will grow into action. Step by step, little by little, we compromise ourselves. We allow sin into our lives until, one day, we wake up and discover that sin has destroyed us, too.

Many Christians start out watching R-rated movies, then X-rated. They gradually progress from softcore to hard-core pornography until they become addicted, trapped by sexual sin. From there, it is a small step to sexual perversions of all kinds. Some homosexuals brag about having hundreds of sexual partners a year. With sexual sin so rampant in our nation, is it any wonder that a disease like AIDS can claim thousands of lives each year?

The cycle of sin

There are two ways you can live your life: in the sin cycle or in the love cycle.

The sin cycle begins when we are born. The Bible says we are all guilty of sin. We are all self-centered and self-seeking. We sin, and guilt, broken relationships, and a sense of emptiness are the results. These lead to poor self-esteem. We don't feel good about ourselves. To compensate, we try to build ourselves up. This results in a dependence on ourselves instead of God. We become egocentric. We lack humility. We want others to hold us in high esteem. Pride guides our lives, and this leads us back to sin and a continuation of the cycle.

How can we break out of the sin cycle? There is only one answer: the love cycle. Jesus said, *"Love the Lord your God with all your heart and with all your soul and with all your mind.... Love your neighbor as yourself"* (Matthew 22:37,39).

The cycle of love

The answer to the sin cycle is Christ's love. Because He loves us, we can love Him with our whole hearts, and His love in us will overflow to others. Because we love God, we try to obey Him, and His Spirit produces the fruit of the Spirit in us—love, joy, peace, longsuffering, gentleness, goodness, meekness, temperance, and faith (see Galatians 5:22).

We no longer have to strive to be superior to others. Instead, our egotism turns into humility. We now want to help others by showing compassion. And as we love others, God fills us with more of His love, and the cycle begins again.

You must make a choice. What do you want to dominate your life: sin or Christ's love? You decide.

Our country is headed for disaster

Unfortunately, our nation today is full of people who are caught in the sin cycle. The 1980s were known as the "Me Decade" because people only cared about themselves. The rule today is: Do your own thing and let the world take care of itself. People are losing their moral values. Anything goes and, because of that, our country is headed for disaster.

What can we as Christians do to save our country? We must get involved, each and every one of us, and work to change things. Elected officials, clergy, educators, workers, parents, the media—every Christian must help. We must work to rid our country of the filth and apathy that is strangling us and reinstate God in the hearts and minds of Americans. If we don't, this country will be devastated in the next decade.

We must show the world that true happiness can only come from God. Sure, sin give happiness but only for a short period of time. But the peace, contentment, and joy that the world seeks can only be found in a right relationship with God.

Our country needs spiritual regeneration as presented in the Bible. We need an old-time revival that will convict people of their sins and bring them to God. As Christians, we need to get off our padded pews and start living for God the way His Word says we are to live. We need to start practicing spiritual breathing. We need to start being the light and salt of the earth, so people will see us and turn to God.

Sin is no joke

Many people will almost cheerfully admit to being sinners because they have no idea what that means. They think sin is another word for human nature and hide behind the fact that everybody does it.

God hates sin. He doesn't hate sinners—He hates sin. He is a holy and just God, and He must punish sin and evil in the world. You can pay the penalty of sin yourself by spending eternity in hell. Or you can accept a substitute in your place—Jesus Christ. Jesus died on the cross and endured God's wrath so we wouldn't have to.

You choose to sin and break God's law. When you deliberately disobey Him day after day and do not repent and change your ways, you are bringing God's judgment against yourself. Some day you will stand before God and He will judge you GUILTY of sin.

God doesn't send anyone to hell. He loves us too much, and He has done everything He can do to keep even one person from going to hell. We choose to go to hell ourselves when we refuse to accept God's substitute, Jesus. God says to you, "Let's make a trade. You give Me all your sins, failures, frustrations, and uncertainty. Then I'll give you:

+ A clean record with every sin forgiven and forgotten forever.
+ Peace of mind.
+ Purpose and direction for living.
+ Life that never ends.
+ Power to cope with every situation.
+ A confirmed reservation in heaven."

All you have to do is accept God's offer...or reject it. YOU have the choice.

118

Chapter 12

Judgment: Men's or God's?

Man was created to have fellowship with God, and nothing else will ever truly satisfy him. We try to fill our lives with material things, with relationships and causes, but still the emptiness remains. The void that only God can fill is still inside us.

When we accept Jesus Christ, God's Holy Spirit comes and lives in us. We are no longer incomplete because God has made us complete. We become new creations. *If anyone is in Christ,* says 2 Corinthians 5:17, *he is a new creation; the old has gone, the new has come!*

The Christian lives by God's law

So how do we live this new life? How do we live as God's people? The answer is, we live according to God's Word. In it He gives us His laws. He tells us what He expects of us and what we can expect of Him.

The law of the Lord is perfect, reviving the soul.

The statutes of the Lord are trustworthy, making wise the simple.

The precepts of the Lord are right, giving joy to the heart.

The commands of the Lord are radiant, giving light to the eyes.

The fear of the Lord is pure, enduring forever.

The ordinances of the Lord are sure and altogether righteous.

They are more precious than gold, than much pure gold; they are sweeter than honey, than honey from the comb.

By them is your servant warned; in keeping them there is great reward (Psalm 19:7-11).

If our lives are to have meaning, purpose, and order, they must be based on God's law. God is the only One who can determine right and wrong. He sets the standards we are to live by. Mankind is too sinful to determine what is right and wrong for himself. Only One who is absolutely pure and perfect can do that.

A lot of people nowadays believe in situational ethics. That means that what is right and what is wrong is determined by the situation. What's wrong in one situation may not be wrong in another situation. It's up to the individual to determine, situation by situation, what his standards are.

Friend, that kind of thinking is inspired by the devil. The Bible warns that people who try to create their own standards and moral laws are going to be judged by God. It doesn't matter if something seems right or wrong to you; the only thing that matters is what God's Word says is right or wrong.

Jesus said, *"I tell you the truth, until heaven and earth disappear, not the smallest letter, not the least stroke of a pen, will by any means disappear from the Law until everything is accomplished"* (Matthew 5:18).

We will all face God's judgment

Some day, you and I will stand before God and He will judge us for the things we've done in this life. I promise you that, on that day, God isn't going to judge you according to what you think is right and wrong. He's going to judge you according to what His Word says is right and wrong.

Hebrews 9:27 says, *Man is destined to die once, and after that to face judgment.* Since my escape from death, I realize more than ever that there is only one true set of standards in this world and it is God's. Sometimes I tremble when I think how God is going to judge this nation for turning its back on His laws.

The Bible states again and again that someday we will all face God's judgment. Every person who has ever lived will stand before Him. In His Word, God tells us that, when that day comes, we will have to give account to Him of all the wrong we have done. God is a God of love and mercy, but He is also a God of judgment.

A lot of people can't handle that. They want to believe that God is too merciful and loving to ever judge anyone and too kind to ever send anyone to hell. But that kind of thinking is wrong.

You see, when God gave mankind free will to choose, He also gave him the right to choose the wrong. Without that choice, there is no free will. And when we choose wrong, we must also pay the price for our wrongdoing.

God is a righteous God. He cannot tolerate sin. It goes against His very nature. He is so holy and pure that He cannot stand sin. God is also just. If we do what is right, we will be rewarded. If we do what is wrong, we must pay the price for our sin. And what is the price of sin? Death and separation from God.

121

Sounds harsh, doesn't it? But it's true. God paid a tremendous price when He granted man free will. He knew there would be many who would choose the wrong instead of the right. And, because God loves us so much, it broke His heart to think of the dreadful price we would have to pay for our wrong. That's why God himself paid the price for our wrongdoing.

We've all done wrong. Not one of us is without sin. We all deserve God's judgment of death and separation. But God so loved the world that he gave His one and only Son, that whoever believes in him shall not perish but have eternal life (see John 3:16).

God loves us so much that He paid the price for our sin. On a cross some 2,000 years ago, Jesus Christ—God's only Son—took the punishment for our sins upon himself. He died in our place. He died for us so that we could live.

If you have accepted Jesus Christ as your Lord and Savior, when you stand before God on Judgment Day, He will look at your record and find you faultless. Stamped over the record of your sins will be "Paid in full by Jesus Christ!" Because Jesus took your punishment, God will not punish you.

Unfortunately, there will be multitudes who did not accept Jesus Christ as Savior. In their time on earth, they rejected God and His Word. They chose to make themselves God, to set their own standards of right and wrong, to live as they pleased. And when they face the righteous judgment of God, He will have no choice but to cast them into hell.

"But why," you ask, "would a merciful God send anyone to hell?"

God doesn't send anyone to hell. People choose to go to hell. God has done everything He can do to make sure that NO ONE goes to hell. He came to this earth, lived among us, and died on the cross to pay the price for our sins. He gave us His Word so we would know what is right and wrong and what He expects of us. He told us over and over again that judgment is coming, that there will be a day of accounting, that we will all stand before Him to be judged, and that it is up to US to choose whether we go to heaven or hell.

And still people refuse to believe. They refuse to accept Jesus Christ and, in doing that, they are choosing to go to hell. God doesn't send them to hell; they choose to go there themselves.

Judgment Day is coming

Today, people discount and ridicule the idea of God's judgment, just as people did in the past. Genesis 6:5-7 says, *The Lord saw how great man's wickedness on the earth had become, and that every inclination of the thoughts of his heart was only evil all the time. The Lord was grieved that he had made man on the earth, and his heart was filled with pain.*

Practically from the beginning, men discounted God's judgment. These people didn't worry about doing wrong. They went about their business, doing just what they wanted to do, without a thought that they were accountable to God for the wrong they were doing. They became so evil that God sent the flood and wiped mankind off the face of the earth, all but Noah and his family.

You say, "Oh, that was a long time ago. People are not like that now."

Really? Jesus said, *"As it was in the days of Noah, so it will be at the coming of the Son of Man* [the end times]. *For in the days before the flood, people were eating and drinking, marrying and giving in marriage, up to the day Noah entered the ark; and they knew nothing about what would happen until the flood came and took them all away"* (Matthew 24:37-39).

We're no different from the people of Noah's day. We go about our business, doing what we want to do, living the way we want to live. We don't worry about God's judgment; we do what WE feel is right or wrong. Most of us don't even think about judgment or death, but death is inevitable for every one of us and judgment is just as certain as death.

People today ridicule the idea of a just and holy God. They laugh at the thought of judgment and hell. They label the virgin birth and the Resurrection myths and declare the Ten Commandments primitive and outdated.

Our society reacts more to a racial, political, or sexual putdown than it does when Christianity, Christ, God, or the Bible are degraded. It's okay to make fun of the Bible on television and to openly break God's laws. Just don't say anything that might be interpreted as a racial, political, or sexual putdown or you're in trouble. Just ask former sports announcer, Jimmy the Greek. He was fired by CBS for his comments about black athletes, which many took as a racial putdown.

You can't say anything bad about homosexuals, adulterers, fornicators, thieves, liars, murderers, etc., in the media, or you will get in serious trouble. Yet, the media degrades Christian beliefs and everything we hold sacred. They discount this nation's religious heritage—the one thing that has made this nation great. At the same time, they promote or condone homosexuality, adultery, stealing, lying, pornography, and every other sin imaginable.

These things do not go unnoticed by God. He knows. He is keeping account of the wrongs. And, some day soon, the great day of reckoning will come. John the Revelator describes it this way:

I saw a great white throne and him who was seated on it. Earth and sky fled from his presence, and there was no place for them. And I saw the dead, great and small, standing before the throne, and books were opened. Another book was opened, which is the book of life. The dead were judged according to what they had done as recorded in the books.

The sea gave up the dead that were in it, and death and Hades [hell] gave up the dead that were in them, and each person was judged according to what he had done.... If anyone's name was not found written in the book of life, he was thrown into the lake of fire (Revelation 20:11-13,15).

We will all be judged and the records will determine where we will spend eternity—in the presence of God in heaven or separated from God in hell. Unfortunately, this is not for a lifetime, a few years or decades, but for eternity, for forever! People who did not want to serve God while on earth will have their wish granted—they will be separated from Him forever!

There is no second chance after death. You must choose NOW where you will spend eternity. John 3:36 says, *Whoever believes in the Son has eternal life, but whoever rejects the Son will not see life, for God's wrath remains on him.*

What will it be—eternal life or eternal death?

Chapter 13

The Death of the American Home

The Christian home is under attack today, not only from the godless society around us but from the very institution that should be protecting it—our government. Lobbying by liberal, anti-God groups has pressured our government representatives to pass or try to pass laws that are in complete opposition to what the Bible declares.

The ERA would have destroyed the home

The Equal Rights Amendment (ERA) was one such law that, fortunately, was not passed (but who knows what the future holds?). Now, don't get me wrong. I believe in equal rights for all Americans without regard for race or sex, but the ERA would not have insured equal rights for all. The way the ERA would have changed the law would have resulted in a devastation of the American family and of morality in this nation. In fact, I believe that the ERA would have caused the death of the American home.

Many feminist groups were pushing for passage of the ERA. These groups don't believe in the traditional family structure. In fact, they don't even believe in marriage because they feel it constitutes virtual slavery for women. Therefore, they feel that freedom for women cannot be won without destroying marriage. And when you destroy marriage you destroy the home.

The feminists want freedom from motherhood and from the responsibility of caring for children. They advocate free day-care centers paid for by the government. But can the government raise children with the same love and discipline that a loving, dedicated mother can give? Can the government match the moral teachings of a mother who is not polluted with liberalism and materialism?

Many communist countries have already tried the day-care approach to raising children. Instead of productive, moral, loving people, they have a generation of godless people who only exist for what the state can give them. They have no ambition or drive, no morals, no community concern, no love for parents or anyone else.

The Christian home is built on relationships with open, constant communication, with parents setting examples and teaching their children, with daily Bible study and prayer, and the development of good moral habits. Godly parents discipline their children when necessary and love them unconditionally and unreservedly.

Children are, in many ways, the products of their environment, and their first few years are extremely critical. That's why we must be careful that we put them in the very best environment possible for learning and growing. This environment should be in the home, not in day-care centers which cannot teach Christian doctrines. The home should be the place where children learn morality, concern for others, love of God, and patriotic duty.

Now, this doesn't mean that I don't believe in child care. Unfortunately, it is often a necessity in today's society. I don't believe, however, that it should ever take the place of the home. Children shouldn't be left in child-care centers from the time they are infants until they start school. The centers simply cannot provide the teaching, nurturing, and example-setting that mothers and fathers provide at home. Even Christian day-care centers cannot provide the one-on-one love and care that a mother provides.

The media presents a false picture

It used to be that mothers were respected and cherished. It was not uncommon to hear someone praise his or her mother for the godly teachings and good upbringing they received. But today women are being put down, misused, and devalued. They are treated like second-class citizens. Worse than that, they are treated like mere sexual objects for the gratification of men.

You can see this portrayal of women everywhere you look in the media today. Cars, candy bars, laundry soap—you name it, and sex is being used to sell it. Women are displayed as sexual objects to sell products.

Think about it. In almost every commercial or ad, you'll see a sexy woman or parts of her anatomy. She flirts with the camera, moves seductively, tries to arouse. And all to sell a product.

Movies and magazines are just as bad. How many popular movies and magazines are out today that portray women as loving, caring, godly mothers? Virtually none. We see women as executives, police-women, workers, criminals, prostitutes, judges, etc., but rarely do we see them as mothers. When we do, more than likely, they are bad mothers or not the kind of mothers we want our children to emulate.

When a movie or magazine does depict a good mother, she is usually a "super-mom." Not only does she bring home the bacon, as the old joke goes, but she cooks it, too. Super-moms do everything and have everything. They nurture their children, are wonderful wives, have fantastic, fulfilling jobs, keep in shape and look great, are concerned about the environment and their communities, are moral, and are downright PERFECT! Unfortunately, no such woman really exists. These aren't realistic portrayals of women, and they demean women by suggesting that perfection is possible.

Many movies and magazines portray women as wives, but they are not of the biblical variety. Most are unfaithful and uncaring. They're angry, hurt, confused, bored, ambitious, scheming, and any other negative thing you can think of. Whatever happened to the old-fashioned wife and mother of our nation's past? Why have such virtues as faithfulness, dedication, love, commitment, self-sacrifice, and responsibility gone out of fashion? And why have men allowed themselves to be suckered by such false and negative portrayals? How many men today are dissatisfied with their wives because they aren't "super-moms" or "super-wives"?

A national cartoon strip recently carried the story line of an executive who divorced his wife of many years to marry a younger woman. The cartoon character explained his actions by saying he *deserved* a young, beautiful, sexy wife. After all, he had worked hard for many years, and now he felt he had *earned* this kind of wife. Besides, his executive friends were all getting younger wives, and he *wanted* one, too. If that isn't treating women as objects, I don't know what is!

Proverbs 5 is a warning against adultery and the kind of mentality this cartoon executive had. Verse 18 says, *May you rejoice in the wife of your youth.* Why? Verse 21-23 says, *For a man's ways are in full view of the Lord, and he examines all his paths. The evil deeds of a wicked man ensnare him; the cords of his sin hold him fast. He will die for lack of discipline, led astray by his own great folly.*

Men who throw away their wives of many years will not go unnoticed—or unpunished—by God. We are to value and love our wives. We are to treat them with respect as our lifelong companions and the mothers of our children.

The Bible's way is best

The Bible tells us how women are to be treated. Ephesians 5:22-33 says, *Wives, submit to your husbands as to the Lord. For the husband is the head of the wife as Christ is the head of the church, his body, of which he is the Savior. Now as the church submits to Christ, so also wives should submit to their husbands in everything.*

Husbands, love your wives, just as Christ loved the church and gave himself up for her to make her holy, cleansing her by the washing with water through the word, and to present her to himself as a radiant church, without stain or wrinkle or any other blemish, but holy and blameless.

In this same way, husbands ought to love their wives as their own bodies. He who loves his wife loves himself. After all, no one ever hated his own body, but he feeds and cares for it, just as Christ does

131

the church—for we are members of his body. "For this reason a man will leave his father and mother and be united to his wife, and the two will become one flesh." This is a profound mystery—but I am talking about Christ and the church. However, each one of you also must love his wife as he loves himself, and the wife must respect her husband.

So many people have the mistaken idea that submission means inferiority and slavery, but that is NOT the case. God designed marriage and the family in the way that it could function best. The wife respects her husband and follows his leading. The husband loves his wife totally and unselfishly, and he has the responsibility before God as the family's spiritual leader.

That's where the problems come in today. We demand that women submit but, as men, we fail to love them totally and unselfishly. We demand that they be and do what we want—not for their good but for our gratification. That's why so many men are walking away from their marriages and deserting their children. It's a national disgrace that so many women and their children are living below poverty level. This should NOT be!

That's one of the reasons why children sit out their childhood in day-care centers. Their fathers have abandoned them, and their mothers have to work full time to support the family. The fathers have forsaken their moral and spiritual obligation as leaders of the home. They are not providing for their families so the mothers CAN stay home and care for the children.

I think it is also a sign of our morally corrupt times that, in many families, both parents have to work full time to provide for their children. We are too materialistic, too concerned with things instead of people. We want to keep up with the Jones instead of being content with what we have.

I'm not saying that all families in which both parents work are morally corrupt. Sometimes, because of sickness or job loss, both parents have to work to make ends meet, but this should be the exception instead of the rule. As Christians, we must work to change our government and society to make it possible for all mothers to stay home with their children. The very future of our nation depends on it!

As the home goes, so goes the nation

Mothers and fathers are so important. God has placed the lives of our children in our hands. We mold them by our love, concern, and example throughout their lives until they grow to be responsible adults, knowing right from wrong. We cannot pass the responsibility for our children on to someone else. God will hold us accountable for how they turn out. That doesn't mean we have to be perfect. It means we should always strive to do our best and to pray daily for God's direction and help.

God will help us. He has provided us a guide—the Bible—that reveals His plan and guidance for living. He has made it very clear, both in the Old and New Testaments, that our children are a gift from Him. They are just loaned to us for a while, and we, as parents, are responsible for teaching them godly standards.

The kind of job we do as parents will affect not only our children but our nation. If we continue to neglect our children as we have been doing for the past several decades, we will continue to see our nation decline, morally and in every way. It is true that as the home goes, so goes the nation. If we allow our

133

homes to be destroyed, our nation will be destroyed as well.

Schools cannot teach morals

An institution cannot teach your children godly standards. Our schools certainly can't. Today they are becoming increasingly humanistic, evolutionary, and atheistic. When we expelled God from our public schools, we also expelled His laws. When the Supreme Court ruled against God, it also destroyed the observing of His standards. The Court ruled that the Ten Commandments could not hang on the walls of our schools. Why? Because the students might read and obey them and that would constitute a violation of the separation of church and state.

A lot of people believe that the separation of church and state is a part of our Constitution, but that is not true. The First Amendment simply states: "Congress shall make no law respecting an establishment of religion or prohibiting the free exercise thereof." Under the banner of religion, you can worship yourself (secular humanism), the devil (Satanism), money (materialism), or anything else, and the government can't stop you.

I don't think today's interpretation of separation of church and state is what our founding fathers were thinking about when they wrote the Constitution. Most were Christians and simply didn't want the government to create a state religion (such as England had), or prohibit people from practicing their religion (as England had done). They never intended for religion to be outlawed in anything connected to the state.

In the beginning, the distance between church and state was small. But from the authoring of the Constitution through all the years and the "interpretations" given it by our courts up until 1960, the distance between church and state has grown steadily. Today we have gone completely (and absurdly) in the opposite direction. In trying to preserve the original intent of the Constitution, we have outlawed anything religious for anything connected with the state.

We have gradually been losing our godly beliefs, which George Washington and Benjamin Franklin believed could and would change the course of this nation. In their writings, these forefathers stated many times that when we lose our God-based values, we would lose our rights, property, and success as people and a nation.

Since God was removed from our schools in the 1960s, our nation's morality has almost disappeared. Surveys show that premarital sex is up over 400 percent. Pregnancies among teenage girls are up 500 percent. Suicides have increased more than 400 percent among students. We now lead the western world in teenage pregnancies, violent crime, divorce, illegal drug use, and abortion.

"I am much afraid that schools will prove to be great gates of hell unless they diligently labor in explaining the Holy Scriptures, engraving them in the hearts of youth. I advise no one to place his child where the Scriptures do not reign paramount. Every institution in which men are not increasingly occupied with the Word of God must become corrupt."

Martin Luther

How did all this happen? Who is really at fault?

135

Over 80 percent of Americans claim a belief in God, yet our moral standards continue to fall. Can we blame all the problems on the courts which made the final rulings? No, the courts only legalized what our communities had been permitting for several years. The truth is, we are all at fault.

Schools were never intended to teach children morals—that has always been the parents' job. Our schools should only reinforce what our children learn at home. They should work together with the parents to teach and train children so they will grow up to be moral, caring, responsible people.

Parents are responsible and will answer to God for providing or not providing a godly education for their children. The job begins at home. Whether the schools help parents do their job or not is not nearly as important as whether or not parents do their job.

That's why mothers are so important. They have the opportunity to share and mold their children's lives in ways no one else can. By spending time with their children in their early years, mothers set the direction for their children's lives. They give their children the most important things they will ever have.

Since World War II, however, our society has shifted its emphasis away from the importance of spiritual and moral training to the shallowness of materialism. During the last three decades, women who stayed at home to care for their families were made to feel unimportant and inferior. They didn't earn any money and, therefore, had no power. They didn't run large corporations or the government, and so what they did was regarded as unimportant. They didn't hold positions of power and prestige, the reasoning went, so they must be incapable of being leaders.

How foolish! That's the way sin twists our thinking. While men were running the world, wives and mothers were home preparing the future. They were doing a job greater than any material compensation. But instead of encouraging and appreciating them, a male-dominated society made them feel that men were somehow superior to them and that what men did was ultimately more important and necessary.

The result was that women began focusing on gaining equality with men in the workplace. If taking care of the home and family was not important, women would no longer do it. They would dedicate themselves to achieving money and power. And no one seemed to realize—until now—that a mother's job is far more important than any success this world has to offer.

Divorce continues to rise. Abortion increases each year. There are more troubled children than ever before. While Mom and Dad are out chasing the almighty dollar, there's no one to stay home with the kids. The statistics show that the American family is decaying due to the changes in our new lifestyle. We refuse to give our children the teaching and training they need at home, and we have made it legally impossible for our schools to do it. No wonder our children feel lost and alone in the world. On the other hand, we thank God for those parents who both must work but still put God first by having daily devotions with their children.

I thank my parents for their teaching and training and for their personal examples. I didn't need to turn to drugs or sin to find the answers for my life because I always had their example to follow. I've made many mistakes but I've always had my Christian training at home to come back to.

Our nation has been great, but we are facing internal decay because we have lost our true values. We've turned away from God and His teachings, and we no longer know what is true and right and good in the world. We no longer value marriage, parenthood, our children and families. And, if we don't stop in the way we're going and turn back to God, the family will someday cease to exist. And when that happens, this nation is doomed. It was built on the family and will die without it.

The damage being done to families today by the government, under the pretense of "human rights," is incredible. Children sue their parents, parents abandon their children, spouses divorce each other. We can say what we want, do what we want, live like we want. It doesn't matter if it hurts our spouses or children. "I" am all that is important.

It's becoming almost a rarity today to find families that don't include stepparents and stepchildren. Divorce rates skyrocket as marriage rates plummet. And while the number of births falls, the illegitimacy rates continue to rise.

What can we do? One thing we must do is elect dedicated Christian men and women to run our nation and make our laws. How can we expect anything but disaster when we have greedy, amoral individuals making the laws for our country? These people's lives are completely out of control. They don't even practice their own ideologies. Yet, they are in positions where they make—or break—laws that affect our families and our nation.

If the time comes—and God forbid that it ever does—when secular humanism completely takes over, everyone will live according to the ungodly principles they have been taught in our schools and by the media. Morality will be ridiculed. Evil will be a virtue. Everyone will do what they feel is right in his own eyes. Standards of right and wrong will be determined by the individual.

When and if that day ever happens, I fear for this country because God will judge us. In the meantime, we continue to head in that direction. We continue to ban God from our schools and eliminate Him from our lives. We continue to remove God from His rightful place of leadership in our lives and set ourselves up as gods.

"Let the religious element in man's nature be neglected, let him be influenced by no higher motives than low self-interest, and subjected to no stronger restraint than the limits of civil authority, and he becomes the creature of selfish passion or blind fanaticism.

"On the other hand, the cumulation of the religious sentiment represses licentiousness, inspires respect for law and authority, and gives strength to the whole social fabric, at the same time that it conducts the human soul upward to the authority of its being."
Daniel Webster, 1851.

We also continue to reap the tragic harvest of our actions: warped minds, rampant drug use, premarital sex, alcoholism, AIDS, murder, child abuse.... The list goes on and on. We try to band-aid the problem with education, but education without morality is meaningless.

139

We teach our children that drugs are bad for them, that sex results in pregnancy and disease, that life is theirs for the taking. Yet, in increasing numbers, they continue to take drugs, get pregnant, and commit suicide. So we offer them more education, free abortion clinics, and suicide counseling. We offer them everything but what they truly need—God and His Word.

Our children today need moral moorings. As a friend of mine once put it, they need a wall to lean on that will not move. They need to know that there are some things that will never change, that God has set the standards of right and wrong and that we will suffer the consequences if we disobey. They need to know that the only things in life that really matter are God and what His Word says.

Our children aren't going to find those things in our immoral schools. They need to learn them at home and then have them reinforced at schools that teach God-given morals. That's why I believe we must fight to have God put back into public education. If we fail to have a godly witness in our public schools, where the majority of our next generation will be trained, then our next generation will be more hostile or apathetic to God than this present generation. And America will be further destroyed.

The great Christian, Pascal, wrote,

"Human things must be known to be loved, but divine things must be loved to be known.

"I have already passed on much of my earthly possessions to my family, but there is one more thing I wish I could give them—

Christian faith. If they had that and I had not given them one cent, they would still be rich. But if I had given them the whole world and they didn't have Christian faith, they would be poor."

This is true for every American family. We may have all the appliances and gadgets available. The average family today has more conveniences and luxuries than the wealthiest kings and nobles of the last century, when such things simply didn't exist. We may give our children the best of everything. We may send then to the best schools and universities. But if we haven't given them a strong Christian faith, they are indeed poor and have nothing. A family that prays and worships God together will grow strong, and as our families grow strong, our nation will again be strong.

Someday, when we take our last breath, I fear we will find that the things we were so proud of in this life are really meaningless in eternity.

I pray that we will all become aware of the truly important things in life and give those things to our children. If we give them a strong faith in God, they will truly have everything they need.

Chapter 14

Why Communism is Still a Threat

With the dramatic events we have witnessed in Eastern Europe and Russia in recent years, a lot of people have the mistaken idea that communism is no longer a threat to this country or the world. Nothing could be further from the truth. Communism is still alive and well in many nations of the world (including the USSR), and communists today are as determined as ever to eventually stamp out Christianity completely.

The irony is that the United States, as a so-called Christian nation, is helping the communists do just that! We are pouring millions of dollars into Russia, China, and other communist-controlled countries, as well as giving them our latest technology, under the guise of pursuing peace. Yet the communists continue to torture and kill untold millions in nations around the world. They have outlawed God and Christian values—the very things that have made our nation great. And if they had the opportunity, they would destroy us today! Yet we continue to support and help them.

Our foreign policy is twisted

A perfect example of our twisted foreign policy is our dealings with South Africa. Here is a country that is unquestionably anti-communist; yet we have placed sanctions against South Africa and encouraged the world to do the same. We are trying to cause the collapse of this nation in the name of equality. We feel the black South Africans are getting a raw deal because they are being ruled by a white minority.

What most Americans don't understand is that if the white government of South Africa is destroyed, the communists will rush in and seize power. And when that happens, you can be sure, it's the end of South Africa. Thousands of Africans—black and white—will die.

Already, most of the nations bordering South Africa are run by communists. The European nations that once controlled these countries were driven out, and the black Africans were allowed to rule themselves. Unfortunately, the people were not adequately prepared for self-government. The communists were strong and they took over. Today, the people of these nations are starving. They have few jobs, no homes, no adequate medical care, and no education. Most are doing everything possible to migrate into South Africa.

How is the United States dealing with this communist threat? While Russia and other communist countries send weapons to the communists in these countries, the United States sends food, clothing, and medicine. Our dealings, of course, are the most humane, but it doesn't take a genius to figure out who will eventually take over complete control of the nations of Africa.

Why should we care?

Why should we care whether or not the communists take over Africa? Because if Africa falls to the communists, our nation's economy and industry will be severely threatened and we will be unable to defend ourselves in a modern war. Over 80 percent of the world's strategic minerals are mined in Africa, including chromium, manganese, and platinum. Zimbabwe (formerly Rhodesia) produces some of the best chromium in the world, with its high content of titanium which is used for making jet engines, rockets, and modern weapons. It also ranks number six in the world in gold production.

If we lose Africa to the communists, we have lost the world. And I believe South Africa is the key to the continent. If South Africa falls, Africa will be ruled by the communists.

Nelson Mandela is NOT a hero

In 1990, Nelson Mandela was released from a South African prison. Many people, including thousands of Americans, see Mandela as a hero, the champion of black Africans, and the defender of freedom in Africa. History has shown, however, that this isn't the case.

Mandela is a leader of the African National Congress (ANC). The ANC is controlled by the South African Communist Party (SACP) which is under the direct control of Joe Slova, a colonel in the Russian secret police. The SACP is a small group of radical blacks who are dedicated to the violent overthrow of the South African government. Nothing less will satisfy them. The SACP is not a majority, but they have convinced the world, via the secular press, that they speak for the majority. This is untrue.

Mandela himself verified the SACP's violent intentions during his 1990 tour of the United States. He believes that the only way to black rule in South Africa is through violence, and that is the reason he was put in prison in the first place. He believes that communists should and will rule that country.

Please understand—the issue here is not whether Mandela is a black man in a white-dominated society. The issue is lawlessness. He was put in prison because he advocated and directed violence against the South African government.

Is anything wrong with that? Well, suppose a well-known American black leader like Jesse Jackson was advocating the overthrow of the United States government by force and led a group which had destroyed a number of government installations. Would we excuse him because he was fighting for the black communist minority in this country? Would we call him a hero because we felt he was trying to do a good thing? And how would we feel if other countries put sanctions on us because we put him in jail?

You say that isn't a good comparison, that blacks in South Africa have suffered more prejudice and mistreatment at the hands of their government than the blacks in our country. Maybe, maybe not. Does that make it okay for Mandela to use violence against the government—and black Africans—because he and others were the victims of violence? I think not.

The media has tried to present Mandela as some kind of savior of the depressed people of Africa. This is in spite the fact that he endorses and encourages violence and praises those who use it, including such terrorists as Kaddafi, Castro, and Arafat. He was given a hero's welcome when he came to our country and was wined and dined at the White House. He was even allowed to address a joint session of Congress.

Mandela is NOT a hero. He is NOT the savior of black Africans. Mandela is a communist. Through the years, he has written many articles advocating communism. In one article, he wrote, "The people of the South African Communist Party will destroy capitalism and build in its place socialism, and it cannot be affected by slow changes but by revolution. The communists must take control of South Africa." Another of his articles was entitled, "How To Be a Good Communist."

Why is our government backing such a man? We know what he advocates and what he stands for. We know why he was imprisoned because the court proceedings are open records. Why are we supporting such a man, when even his own people do not support him?

The media would have us believe that the majority of black South Africans are in agreement with Mandela and support him, but that is simply not true. When he was released from prison, less than 100,000 of his followers showed up, and many of those were from outside the country. Yet, at the very same time, over two million black people in South Africa came out to celebrate Easter and the resurrection of Jesus Christ. They wanted to show the world that the majority of South African blacks are NOT followers of Nelson Mandela. They want a peaceful resolution to the class and power struggles in their country.

By placing sanctions on South Africa, we are only hurting the people of South Africa whom we want to help the most—the blacks—and are helping the communists. We are also hurting ourselves. We refuse to buy certain imports from South Africa, so the imports are sold to other countries who sell them to Russia. Then we buy them from Russia, who makes a 500 percent profit. We're hurting the ones we want to help and helping the ones we want to hurt.

Zimbabwe, Zambia, Mozambique, and other nations surrounding South Africa, hate that nation, but they are dependent on it for their survival. They need the equipment, technology, food, jobs, etc., which they can get in South Africa. Their communist governments are corrupt. The wealth of these nations has ended up in the hands of a few leaders, and nothing is left for the people. Yet South Africa is being blamed for these nations' economic problems. Why?

South Africa has not pillaged these surrounding nations. It hasn't asked for their help or depended on them for anything.

South Africa has the best, most modern army of any nation in Africa. It has a thriving economy and strong industry. It has the ability to produce and manufacture many of its own needed goods, and it produces almost two-thirds of the world's gold. Do we really expect our sanctions to work against a country like that?

South Africa is making racial advancements

We must remember that South Africa did not create its race problems. It inherited them from the British Empire. South Africa did not become a nation until 1961. In the past few decades, South Africa has made great advances in race relations, but the world writes it off as "too little too late!" That isn't fair. Before we judge another country, perhaps we should look at our own civil rights movement and the condition our minorities are in today. The truth is, there are no easy answers or solutions to their racial problems or our own.

The racial problem in South Africa is particularly complex. Tribalism is very strong, so strong that it cuts across national boundaries and goes back hundreds of years. Tribal hatreds and conflicts account for the deaths of thousands of black Africans each year. In fact, most of the blacks killed in South Africa each year are killed by other blacks, not by whites. Yet the whites are always blamed. Why? Is it because the thought of blacks killing blacks goes against our idea of the downtrodden black masses being killed and persecuted by the white minority?

The South African government is changing. The ruling minority is trying to work out a peaceful and acceptable solution to the problems. Already, 34 of South Africa's original 36 apartheid laws have been abolished. And that nation, with less than 10 percent of Africa's total population, has more black million-aires, doctors, and professional people than the rest of Africa put together.

Every year, one-and-a-half million blacks flee from bordering nations into South Africa. If this nation is so bad and conditions are so terrible for blacks, why are these people fleeing their communist countries and coming to South Africa? And why doesn't the United States media give us the truth about the situation?

Our media plays up the "horrible" conditions in South Africa, although that nation has the best standard of living for blacks in all of Africa. They have very little to say about the horrible conditions in neighboring communist countries or the way thousands of black Africans are being killed and tortured by the communists and other tribesmen. What are their motives?

Why does our liberal press want to create another socialist state by destroying South Africa, when recent events have demonstrated how hideous conditions in a socialist state are?

A Soviet admission of failure

Even leaders in the USSR, who once believed in and supported communism, are now saying it doesn't work. Look at this quote by Lennart Meri, Estonia's foreign minister:

"When you shut people's mouths so they cannot talk, when you close their eyes by forbidding them to travel, when you plug their ears by jamming airwaves, the population becomes very passive. In this condition, when people don't care, it seems as if nature herself reacts: fields produce less wheat, forests die of pollution, fouled rivers catch fire. The entire society degrades. This catastrophe is so far unrecognized in the West, but it has been obvious here. Life expectancy has fallen, and the infant mortality rate has risen to its highest level.

"Even the ability of students to learn has deteriorated. Today's technology is so exact and refined that only a person who thinks freely and critically can use it well—a person who has been taught since age four that he has individual worth, who has been taught by age eight that he has rights and responsibilities....

"The rest of the world has evolved, but we have gone backward. This is the tragic difference between the Soviet Union and the rest of the world" *(National Geographic,* November 1990, Vol. 178, No. 5, pg. 10).

Is this the kind of fate we want for South Africa? I pray to God it isn't!

Our secular, humanistic, atheist media report the skirmishes between some South African blacks throwing rocks at government soldiers, but they fail to tell us about the thousands of blacks (mostly moderates and Christians who disagree with the communists' radical approach) who have been murdered by the "death by necklace" method of the communists. This particularly grotesque method of execution was openly endorsed by Nelson Mandela's wife, Winnie, who was awarded the Third-World Peace Prize for her "achievements" in South Africa.

For "death by necklace," a victim's hands are cut off and wire is used to tie his wrists together. A rubber tire is then placed over his shoulders and filled with oil. The oil is ignited and, as the temperature increases, the rubber melts and burns into the victim's flesh. It can take up to 20 minutes for a victim to die.

During just one three-month period recently, approximately 200 deaths occurred in this manner, committed by black communists against South African Christians or moderate blacks. Has our press reported these horrible killings to us? No! Instead, our government continues to bury its head in the sand and give the ANC millions of dollars in support. It continues to support Nelson and Winnie Mandela, who endorse and call for this kind of brutal violence against their black countrymen.

I believe the Mandelas have proven themselves to be communist murderers who will stop at nothing to bring communist ideology into power in South Africa. I do not say these things because they are black. I would feel the same way if they were white, yellow, red—any color. Yet some who read this will label me a racist for my views. But that's not so, because I love all my black brothers in Christ. However, I believe that what the Mandelas and their followers are doing is WRONG! "Two wrongs don't make a right," as the old saying goes, and they cannot justify their violence with the violence of the past.

What about communist countries?

Instead of going after a country like South Africa, why don't we put sanctions on communist nations like Russia, China, and others? You say, "We have put sanctions on these countries." Have we? Maybe a few, but we still continue to pour millions of dollars in aid to these communist countries. We still continue to give them our technology and help, despite the fact that they have slaughtered millions, raped countries of their industries and resources, and enslaved their peoples for decades.

Why do we continue to help them? Do we really think that, if we were in need, the communists would help us?

Russia's Brezhnev Doctrine of 1973 stated, "We will take the oil from the Middle East. We will grab the strategic minerals from South Africa. Then we will dictate the terms of surrender to the United States and the West." Don't let the latest reports on Russia's change of attitude fool you. Before we continue to give Russia and the countries of Eastern Europe billions of dollars, let's see how serious they are about democracy.

I think the communist leaders of these countries are retreating, not surrendering. They are giving up their power because they are being forced to, not because they want to. They haven't had a change of heart, realizing that communism is wrong and democracy is right. They are giving up their power only because the people have taken it from them.

China's communist leaders proved this in 1989. They say they are the voice of the people, that they represent the people's wishes. Yet, when the people of China rose up in protest and demanded change, they were slaughtered by the thousands. The protesters were not asking for an end to communism; they were only asking for the corruption in their government to end. And for that they were murdered, imprisoned, executed, and driven underground.

Even so, we continue to sell our technology and resources to this godless nation. Yet, we can't blame American companies only for this mass giveaway of technology. The blame must also fall on the shoulders of our government which sets the rules and the example.

Even now, the U.S. government is permitting a supercomputer sale to Russia involving technology six times more advanced than originally agreed to. Control Data Corporation will make the $40 million sale, financed by American banks that are secured by the U.S. government.

Common sense tells us that such a transaction will end up being a gift to the USSR, as we know that Russia will never pay the debt. Almost weekly there is a news report of our government forgiving millions of dollars of debts to countries all over the world. How can we afford to do this when we have become the largest debtor nation in the world?

Right here in the United States, we have men like the late Armand Hammer who championed the cause of communism. Mr. Hammer thought communism was so great, but he wouldn't move to Russia. Why not? Because the Russian government doesn't tolerate millionaires. So he continued to live in our free nation where he could make his millions and use them to help communism.

When Mr. Hammer was charged with corruption, was he sent to prison? No, because our President at that time pardoned him. Why? Why do people like him go unpunished? For years, he helped the Russians obtain vital information in exchange for treasures seized from the countries they had overrun. Why was he allowed to get away with it?

On the other hand, we have men like Oliver North, who tried his best to do what his commanding officers wanted done, and he was punished and maligned by the press for it. For trying to help in the fight against communism in South America, he was condemned and disgraced by our government. Isn't there something wrong here? We pardon our criminals and punish our heroes. Is this the America founded under God?

When will we wake up and realize that America is the best nation of the world to live in because it was founded on Christianity? When will we stop helping the communists and start exposing them for what they are? I pray that it isn't too late.

Russia's goals have not changed

The failure of communism has wreaked moral and economic havoc in Russia and forced its leadership to make some changes to appease its angry, deprived people. Even though they have had to seek outside help to feed their citizens and revamp their economy, the long-range militaristic goals of the soviets has not changed. Ultimately, Russia would like to control the mineral wealth of South Africa and the crucial oil reserves of the Persian Gulf.

It is no secret that America needs oil to keep our

industries and transportation systems operating. We import billions of dollars worth of oil each year. On the other hand, Russia is not a large scale oil importer as she has enough domestic supplies.

Why, then, is our government negotiating with the Soviet Union to give away much of the Aleutian Islands territory and five islands off the Alaskan coast? The islands of Herald, Wrangell, Jeannette, Henrietta, and Bennett comprise more than a thousand-mile-wide stretch of oil-rich seabeds which could yield multi-billion barrels of oil. Yet the deal, which is being kept very hush-hush by the state department, is supposedly scheduled to be considered for ratification sometime in 1991.

Why would we give so much oil to Russia? One rationale might be that, since American companies would never be allowed to drill in the area because of political pressure from the environmentalists, the mineral-rich area is being traded for political purposes.

This is madness. When Russia becomes the owner, she will drill for oil with no regard for environmental concerns. The oil will then be sold—probably back to the U.S. at a hefty profit, costing America billions of dollars!

If you are as concerned about this as I am, contact your legislators and voice your opinion. Ask what is behind this crazy giveaway. We have proven that we are willing to risk multiplied thousands of American lives and risk national bankruptcy to insure that the Arabs have oil to sell to us. But why are we willing to give rich oil fields to Russia?

For years, Russia sold arms to Iraq and had approximately nine thousand technical advisors stationed at eight Iraqi military bases. During "Operation Desert

Shield," the U.N.-sanctioned blockade imposed in response to Saddam Hussein's naked aggression against Kuwait and his planned invasion of Saudi Arabia, Russia gave lip service to the plan and basked in the international positive media attention she received.

But the nine thousand technical advisors kept working for the Iraqis! The Russians said they were under contract to teach them how to use the modern weapons they had sold and it would be wrong to break the contracts.

I believe the Russians helped plan the invasion of Kuwait. In July 1990, just a month before Saddam's forces crushed and raped their oil-rich neighbor, Russia's General Albert Mikhaylovich Makashov was sent to Iraq. He is the top soviet expert on tactical warfare. The purpose of his visit now seems obvious.

I was outraged to see Russia, who did not contribute one red ruble or send a single soviet soldier to help in the allied war effort, work hard for a cease fire and peace plan that would salvage Saddam Hussein's pride and enhance Russia's influence in the Middle East.

During the war, we learned that our government had accumulated detailed information about Iraq and the surrounding area. Our intelligence information was excellent—so good that we could destroy the fifth largest army in the world with only slight losses.

How is it possible that our government, the United Nations, and the international media was unaware of Russia's real role in the conflict? Why was it not reported? Why weren't the American people told the truth?

It is very possible that the world's eyes are being blinded to the truth in preparation for the final fulfillment of God's prophetic plan. Students of Bible prophecy realize that the scriptures teach that Russia will be the nation that leads an international army to invade Israel. As I understand it, there is no known biblical reference to the United States. Could it be that, at that time, America will be just another fallen nation that destroyed itself from within? God help us!

My visit to Russia

In the summer of 1990, I was privileged to accompany Bill Bright, founder of Campus Crusade for Christ, on a trip to Russia to premiere the epic movie, "Jesus," in Moscow and Leningrad. What I saw in Russia moved me deeply—I've never been so stirred. And I'll never forget what I saw in that vast, needy nation.

The legacy of communism—its bleakness of life— is seen everywhere. Empty buildings were everywhere, yet there is a desperate housing shortage. A family might wait years for an apartment, then join two other families in a three-bedroom flat, sharing a small kitchen and bathroom.

The shortage of food and clothing is unbelievable, and even when available, the quality of the items is very poor. Russians must stand in line to buy everything, and after waiting for hours, they find the supply is exhausted and there is nothing left.

The ride from the airport into Moscow was fascinating, as our car passed row after row of high-rise apartments built in the early 60s for propaganda purposes, to demonstrate the prosperity of the Russian people. But it is only a facade—a block behind the high-rises, peasants live in squalor.

Despite the grim, survival-level quality of life, the majority of average Russians we talked with were not as concerned about having better food, clothing, and housing as they were in finding something to fill the void in their hearts! After 74 years without access to the Bible and the freedom to worship God, there is a deep spiritual hunger.

I heard of a man who was desperate to learn about God. Finding no one where he lived who could help him, he traveled many miles to Moscow. But he could find no one there who could minister to him. So the man made his way to the U.S. Embassy and asked if anyone there could help him. Alas, they turned him away also, still hungry for the Lord. Finally, the poor man met a Christian who was able to tell him the old, old story about God's love and the Savior's sacrifice for his sins. His face aglow with the thrill of his discovery, the man cried out to God and accepted the Lord Jesus into his heart!

Although several organizations are now taking advantage of new soviet laws and are distributing millions of Bibles and Scripture portions, the need is enormous. There are 285 million people in the Soviet Union, and Bibles have been forbidden for nearly two generations. The spiritual thirst of Russia's masses is even greater than their physical hunger.

In Leningrad, we attended an evangelistic crusade sponsored by Campus Crusade of Europe. More than twenty thousand people jammed into the stadium to hear Kalevi Lehtinen of Finland, sometimes called the Billy Graham of East Europe. He preached a simple message on love—God's love—and gave an invitation for people to come to Christ. Seventeen thousand people went forward, many of them literally running to pray and make a commitment to the Lord.

I was sitting with the small group of Americans Bill Bright had brought with him to Russia. I'm sure there wasn't a dry eye among us. This was one of the most emotionally-moving events of my whole life.

Following the premiere of the "Jesus" film in Leningrad, we were invited to a banquet attended by the mayor, along with several Russian actors and movie producers. I could speak no Russian and most of the people spoke little English. My contact with them was limited to nods, smiles, and handshakes. I had begun to wonder why I had traveled halfway around the world to share my testimony when I was unable to communicate.

I moved out of the way, and was standing at the end of a large table, simply observing. Then, a big Russian man came walking toward me, smiling broadly. He called over a professional interpreter, who let me know the man, Mr. Menaker Leonid, wanted to talk with me. I learned later that he was one of the top officials in charge of all cinema in Russia.

I asked his opinion of the "Jesus" film, which depicts the life, teaching, miracles, persecution, crucifixion, and resurrection of Christ, based on the Gospel of Luke. He said it wasn't that impressive to him—that it was just another movie.

I silently asked God to speak something through me to reach this man's heart, then began to witness to him. I asked if his grandparents or parents were dead, and if he thought he would live forever. If not, was he prepared to face death...where would he spend eternity?

He replied that thinking about death made him unhappy—that he wanted joy in his heart.

For the next few minutes, I shared my testimony—how I dropped dead from heart failure and was restored to life. I explained how I felt God had given me a second chance at life and that my whole mission now is to help others accept the Lord. I told him that, although I was an electrical engineer and had enjoyed much professional success, no achievements or possessions could compare with having a personal relationship with Christ that would last for all eternity.

Mr. Leonid asked the interpreter to have me continue. "No one has ever talked like this to me before," he said.

So I continued to witness. I ended by saying that Jesus could do for him everything He had done for me. I asked if he was ready to stand before God, and stressed that he should make a decision then, because he might never get a second chance.

Suddenly, this big man threw his arms around me, gave me a great bear hug and several Russian kisses on each cheek. He said, "You have touched my heart greatly."

"Only Christ can touch your heart and change you forever, for all eternity," I replied.

"Oh," he said, "I have God and Jesus in my heart... I just can't put Him on my tongue!"

What a gratifying experience. I got my new Russian friend's address and promised to send him a copy of this book as soon as it was finished.

Pray for the Russian people

Pray that God will continue to give another chance to the Russian people to turn from atheistic communism and accept Christ. I believe a great revival can sweep across that huge nation and win millions of precious souls to the kingdom of God.

The godless communist leaders are now realizing that a society cannot exist without a vital religious influence. Their seven-decade experiment helped bring about the complete devastation of their people. They now openly admit that Russia needs new moral bearings to help combat rising alcoholism, a ruined work ethic, and staggering moral problems.

At the same time, America's liberal educators, politicians, attorneys, organizations like the ACLU, the media, and other groups are working hard, promoting the idea that we don't need God in our lives anymore. How can they be so blind?

The "Jesus" film has been shown in theaters all across Russia, and has even been screened in many schools. Ironically, this could never happen in the United States. A film about the life of Christ would be banned for "violating" the so-called constitutional separation of church and state—a concept never intended by our nation's founding fathers.

Pray for Russia. But at the same time, pray for America that we will not become a godless society and lose our freedoms to the secular humanist society. God help us to turn back to Him and not plunge into the dark abyss for which we seem to be headed at breakneck speed.

Chapter 15

The Founding of America

* * * * * * * * * * * * * * * * *

DO YOU KNOW THE ANSWERS
TO THESE QUESTIONS?

1. What type of government controls America today?

2. What type of government was established by our founding fathers?

3. What is the difference between the two?

* * * * * * * * * * * * * * * * *

I have asked these questions of hundreds of Americans and found, to my surprise, that only about five individuals knew the answers. Our founding fathers felt strongly that our nation should be a republic and even stated that if our nation ever became a democracy America would cease to exist.

One of the most popular myths being promoted today in our country is the "separation of church and state." We are told this means that the government—

including federal, state, and local governments—shall not have anything to do with the promotion of religion. The government exists independently of any and all religious concerns.

The people who promote this myth would have us to believe that our nation has never, in any way, supported religion. They say the founders of our nation and those who wrote our laws and Constitution wanted the Church (religion/God) and the State (government) to be separate things. One is not to have anything to do with the other.

This is a MYTH! It isn't true. Our nation and laws were founded upon principles from the Bible. Over and over again the creators of our nation reiterated their belief in God and their dependence on Him. Just a brief look at our history will prove this to be the case.

The first colonists were Christians

The United States began as a sanctuary for people who wanted to worship God in their own way and who were being persecuted for their religious beliefs. They fled to America, where they found peace and freedom to worship as they pleased.

Even the explorer, Christopher Columbus, who is credited for discovering our continent, attributed his success to God. In one of his documents he wrote:

"It was the Lord who put into my mind (I could feel His hand upon me) the fact that it would be possible to sail from here to the Indies. All who heard of my project rejected it with laughter, ridiculing me. There is no question that the inspiration was from the Holy Spirit, because He com-

forted me with rays of marvelous inspiration from the Holy Scriptures....

"I am a most unworthy sinner, but I have cried out to the Lord for grace and mercy, and they have covered me completely. I have found the sweetest consolation since I made it my whole purpose to enjoy His marvelous presence. For the execution of the journey to the Indies, I did not make use of intelligence, mathematics, or maps. It is simply the fulfillment of what Isaiah had prophesied....

"No one should fear to undertake any task in the name of our Savior, if it is just and if the intention is purely for His holy service. The working out of all things has been assigned to each person by our Lord, but it all happens according to His sovereign will, even though He gives advice. He lacks nothing that it is in the power of men to give Him. Oh, what a gracious Lord, who desires that people should perform for Him those things for which He holds himself responsible! Day and night, moment by moment, everyone should express their most devoted gratitude to Him."

In 1620, the purpose of the pilgrims was to establish a government based on the Bible in New England. The charter signed by King James I confirmed the goal to advance the enlargement of Christian religion to the glory of God almighty.

From our nation's beginning, people flocked to

this land to find religious freedom. In 1683, the American colonies reaffirmed their central belief in God in a declaration which states: "We submit our persons, lives, and estates unto our Lord Jesus Christ, the King of kings and Lord of lords, and to all those perfect and most absolute laws of His given us in His Holy Word."

Those "absolute laws" became the basis of our Declaration of Independence and our Constitution. The very basis of our nation was established upon the "absolute laws" of the Bible. Our forefathers did not create our nation based on ungodly officials and the changing ideas of the people but upon the unchanging, just laws that God himself had ordained in His Word.

In the 1700s, a mighty move of God swept across our land and Europe. Great revivals were held throughout the colonies, and many thousands gave their hearts and lives to God. George Whitefield, Francis Asbury, and other great preachers led the revival here, while John and Charles Wesley were instrumental in the great revival which swept England. Thousands upon thousands were brought into the kingdom of God.

Ben Franklin and George Whitefield became close friends during this time and remained good friends until George's death in 1770. This godly man had considerable influence on Franklin, who was one of the key persons in the creation of our nation.

On July 4, 1776, fifty-six courageous men signed the Declaration of Independence and again declared their dependence on God's governing. They proclaimed their independence from England and their continuing dependence upon almighty God. The Declaration states:

"With a firm reliance on the protection of divine providence, we mutually pledge to each other our lives, our fortunes, and our sacred honor."

All the signers of the Declaration expressed their reverence and love for God. They spoke of and referred to Him as their Creator and Judge, and they acknowledged Him as the Protector of their, and our, nation's future.

During this time, a Presbyterian minister was a member of the Continental Congress and president of Princeton University. He was a strong moral and spiritual influence on the other members of Congress through his prayers, his personal witness, and his sharing of moral, biblical principles.

Our Constitution is based on belief in God

In 1787, eleven years after the Declaration of Independence was written, representatives of the 13 colonies gathered in Philadelphia to draft our new nation's Constitution. As the men worked on the agreement that would unite them as a nation, tempers began to flare. The discussion became increasingly bitter, and the meeting was on the verge of collapse. Everything became hopelessly deadlocked.

Finally, Ben Franklin, the elder statesman, arose and said quietly:

"Mr. Chairman, I perceive that we are not in a position to pursue this business any further. Our blood is too hot. I therefore move you, sir, that we separate for three days, during which time, with a conciliatory spirit, we talk with both parties. If we ever

167

make a constitution, it must be the work of compromise.

"While I am on my feet I move you, sir, and I am astonished that it has not been done before, for when we signed the Declaration of Independence we had a chaplain to read the Bible and to pray daily; and I am now moved that when we meet again we have a chaplain to meet with us and invoke the blessing of heaven. For, sir, it has been wisely written, 'Except the Lord build the city, they labor in vain who build it,' and if it be true that a sparrow cannot fall to the ground without His notice, surely a nation cannot rise without His aid."

We are told that George Washington's face beamed with joy as he rose to second the motion.

Franklin's speech energized the minds of the men present to set aside their own priorities and to reach an accord on our Constitution, which has been called the "greatest document ever struck from the brain of man."

When the Constitution was written, it provided for individual religious freedom. It tried to safeguard that liberty by creating the executive, legislative, and judicial branches of government to watch over each other. Their purpose was to keep America from tyranny and to prevent government from taking away people's religious rights. The Constitution was based on Christianity, which meant freedom OF religion—not freedom FROM religion.

Our forefathers never intended our government to outlaw Christianity in schools and city activities. They were trying to protect religious freedom, not do away with it. I believe our constitutional framers never had that intent in mind.

After George Washington became our nation's first president, one of his first official acts was to proclaim a national day of Thanksgiving. His Thanksgiving proclamation reads in part: "Whereas it is the duty of all nations to acknowledge the providence of almighty God and to obey His will, to be grateful for His benefits and humbly implore His protection and favor...." The document goes on to call the nation to thankfulness to God for all the good He has bestowed on our country.

Washington served as president for eight years. In his farewell address he stated:

"Of all the dispositions and habits which lead to political prosperity, religion and morality are indispensable supports. Let us with caution indulge the supposition that morality can be maintained without religion. Reason and experience both forbid us to expect that national morality can prevail in exclusion of religious principles."

How true! If only we could learn this all-important fact that our nation cannot continue to be a moral, just nation when we have removed religion and the basis for that morality from our laws and lives. Proverbs 14:34 says, *Righteousness exalts a nation, but sin is a disgrace to any people.*

We've gone to the other extreme

Today, our courts have gone completely in the opposite direction from what our forefathers envisioned for this nation. Instead of protecting religious and

Christian freedom, our courts have practically out-lawed it. Not only that, they have endorsed humanism and evolution and made them the only "religions" allowed in our schools.

You say, "Oh, humanism and evolution are not religions."

Yes, they are, but instead of God as the object of worship, man is the central figure of their beliefs.

Clarence Darrow argued at the 1925 Scopes "monkey" trial that, under the freedom of religion granted by the Constitution, evolution must be taught in all public institutions. He said it was bigotry to only teach creation. Darrow didn't win the trial by proving evolution was an accepted theory, but he did win the case on the principle of freedom of choice.

How times have changed! Today we no longer have a choice. God and Creationism have been re-moved from the classroom and, thanks in large part to the American Civil Liberties Union (ACLU), evolution is the ONLY view of creation taught to our children in the classrooms of America.

By removing God from our classrooms, the ACLU and our Supreme Court have all but destroyed the Judeo-Christian moral foundation of this nation. And because of it, we are reaping a harvest of drugs, sex, and pregnancy among teens, pornography, disease, crime, and open rebellion. We have a generation that has no regard for themselves, others, or God.

Secular Humanism is the new god

America would never have become great without its Christian basis. In spite of that, many people in government, education, and business have today turned to secular humanism and away from Christianity. Humanism is a complete denial of God. Instead of

GOD being mankind's only hope, humanism says MAN is his own only hope for salvation. And no civilization or nation built on the "goodness" of man has ever survived. When a nation turns its back on God, it ceases to be the best and the greatest. I think we are seeing that happen in America.

But that is not the way our nation's founders intended it to be. Can you imagine our Supreme Court handing down a decision today like the one handed down in 1892 in the "Church of the Holy Trinity vs. the United States"? The Court stated:

"Our laws and our institutions must necessarily be based upon and embody the teachings of the Redeemer of mankind. It is impossible that it should be otherwise; and in this sense and to the extent our civilization and our institutions are emphatic Christians, this is a religious people. This is historically true from the discovery of this continent to the present hour.

"There is a single voice making this affirmation. We find everywhere a clear recognition of the same truth. These and many other matters which might be noticed add a volume of organic utterances that this is a Christian nation."

I simply cannot imagine our Supreme Court today ever making a decision comparable to this one. We have several ultra-liberal judges sitting on the Court whose decisions have drastically affected this nation. I wonder what their defense will be when they

171

someday stand before God and have to give an accounting of their actions on this earth.

I wouldn't want to be in their shoes on that day. Not only will they have to account for their own lives, but they will have to account for the multiplied millions of people who have been affected by their humanistic decisions. They will have to defend to Almighty God why they have pushed Him out of everything and outlawed the very principles and beliefs that once made our nation great.

Over and over again, our Supreme Court justices confirm the constitutionality of the separation of Church and State, but it simply isn't true. Daniel Webster, a great American statesman in the 1800s, once stated:

"Our ancestors established their system of government on morality and religious sentiment. Moral habits, they believed, cannot be trusted on any other foundation than religious principles, nor any government be secure which is not supported by moral habits."

Why do our Supreme Court justices today feel that they are so much more intelligent and enlightened than our great national leaders of the past? How can they honestly believe in separation of Church and State, when it has been so obviously and thoroughly refuted in the past? No wonder our nation is in a moral and legal crisis today. When our laws are no longer based on the unchangeable laws of God, they are subject to every theoretical whim of whomever is in power.

Many of our presidents have supported our Christian heritage. Calvin Coolidge stated:

"The foundation of our society and our government rests so much on the testimony of the Bible that it would be difficult to support them in faith if these teachings would cease to be practically universal in our country."

John Quincy Adams wrote:

"The first and almost only book deserving of universal attention is the Bible."

Abraham Lincoln stated:

"All the good from the Savior of the world is communicated through this Book. But for the Book we would not know right from wrong. All things desirable to man are contained in it."

Woodrow Wilson wrote:

"The Bible is the only supreme source of revelation of the meaning of life, the nature of God, and the spiritual nature and need of men. It is the only guide of life which really leads the spirit in the way of peace and salvation."

James Adams, one of the writers of the Constitution, stated that America must be governed by the Ten Commandments. Yet, today, ungodly men in our government have declared the Commandments too religious and will prosecute anyone for posting them in our schools. In spite of this, the Ten Commandments still remain an important part of our nation's religious heritage. A copy of them hangs over the head of the chief justice of the Supreme Court even today.

Daniel Webster also wrote:

"The moral principles and precepts contained in the Scriptures ought to form the basis of all our civil constitutions and laws. All the miseries and evils which men suffer from—vice, crime, ambition, injustice, oppression, slavery, and war—proceed from their dispersing or neglecting the precepts contained in the Bible."

Do these statements from our past statesmen and leaders sound anything like the statements of our present leaders? Unfortunately, they do not. There is one fundamental truth our current leaders are forgetting: Our nation is great because it was established on godly principles, and when these godly principles are discarded, America will no longer be the greatest nation in the world. In fact, she will cease to exist. We enjoy our civil liberties today solely because our nation was founded upon the beliefs and principles of Jesus Christ.

Every coin minted in our country has the words "In God We Trust" on them. In all that our founding fathers attempted to do, they always sought God's will. We have a great Christian heritage, and if we ever lose it we will lose our greatness as a nation.

Even most of our historic and patriotic songs refer to the fact that America was founded on God and His Word. Our Pledge of Allegiance states, "one nation under God." Yet, today there are individuals who would go so far as to even ban the mention of God in these songs and in the pledge.

Thomas Jefferson once said:

"Can the liberties of a nation be secure when we remove the conviction that our liberties are the gift of God? My God, how little do my countrymen know what precious blessings they are in possession of, and which no other people on earth enjoy!"

I believe the rulings of our Supreme Court and legislators are not valid if they contradict God and the teachings of the Bible. Whether we want to believe it or not, we are under God's law—not above it. The Bible, more than the Constitution, has influenced all our founding documents and is the one determining factor which has made America great.

We are a republic, not a democracy

In our Constitution, the United States is referred to as a republic. Few Americans know that there is a tremendous difference between a republic (founded under God) and a democracy. Our founding fathers said **democracy was an enemy to free people!** Both Alexander Hamilton and James Madison wrote in the *Federalist Papers* that democracies were "turbulence and contention with no personal security."

When our Constitution was drafted, our founding fathers rejected democracy in favor of a republic. Why? How are they different? Officials in both kinds of government are selected by a majority vote. In a **REPUBLIC**, however, elected officials govern according to laws, and government cannot use its power

175

to force the people to do things which are contrary to God's law. The law is over the civil government, just as it is over the individuals.

After signing the Declaration of Independence, Samuel Adams wrote:

"We have this day restored the Sovereign to whom all men ought to be obedient, and from the rising to the setting of the sun, let His kingdom come."

DEMOCRACY, on the other hand, could decide that your property, liberty, and even your very life were the possessions of the majority and could be disposed of without your consent, in any way the will of the majority agreed upon. For example, if the majority of the people were poor, they could use the power of the government to confiscate the riches of the wealthy. If the majority was wealthy, they could pass laws to oppress the poor and deny them their God-given freedoms.

Despite the historical fact that our nation's founding fathers *despised* such democratic power and established a constitutional republic, our nation is referred to as a democracy by many historians and government officials who should know the difference. In fact, most Americans don't even know the difference because the truth of this crucial distinction has been removed from our textbooks—I believe, deliberately. I myself didn't know until I began to study about it.

Our nation has prospered more than any other nation in the world for over 200 years. Many countries look to us as an example. Unfortunately, they think our prosperity is due to a democratic form of government instead of the real reason—because we were a republic founded under God's laws.

In 1843, Willard could honestly write:

"The government of the United States is acknowledged by the wise and good of other nations to be the most free, impartial, and righteous government in the world. But all agree that for such a government to be sustained many years, the principles of truth and righteousness, taught in the Holy Scriptures, must be practiced. The rulers must govern in the fear of God and the people obey its laws."

Although our forefathers started this nation as a constitutional republic, recognizing God as supreme over all matters, we now refer to ourselves as a democracy. We have pushed God out of our thinking and out of our national conscience. We allow ungodly people to make the laws for our nation, without divine guidance from God, the Father of this country.

Under our new "democracy" we eliminated God and prayer from our educational institutions. Under the original republican form of government, this could never have happened, as God was supreme.

For example, in 1973, five members of our Supreme Court sanctioned the right for abortion. The result since then has been the deaths of 30 million unborn children, with more being killed every day. That's more deaths than all the men who have died in all our wars, including the Civil War, World Wars I and II, the Korean War, and the Vietnam War. Does the fact that the Supreme Court sanctioned abortion make it okay? NO! God says it isn't okay, and His law should take precedence over any law of man.

We will never re-establish our republic until we have a spiritual revival and put God back in charge of our nation and our government. If we continue to eliminate God from our lives and country, our liberties will turn into slavery and our nation will be destroyed.

After several years of prosperity, Americans have begun to think we are responsible for creating our blessings and freedoms and have pushed God out of the picture completely. This might be acceptable if Christianity were nothing more than the Ten Commandments—but Christianity is Jesus Christ, born of a virgin, crucified, resurrected, ascended into heaven and living today sovereign over all.

Our nation will never be the great nation it once was until we acknowledge that our greatness comes from God.

Where do we begin to do that? With ourselves. Christianity cannot be just another routine item on our agendas. It must control our thinking and daily behavior. We have to live it. We have to stand up in the face of the majority and proclaim that no law is just and binding unless it is God's law. We have to vote our ungodly leaders out of office and put in men and women who live for and are dedicated to Jesus Christ. Then, and only then, will things begin to change.

America's past is Christian. Its present is humanistic. Its future is up to you.

What about you? Whom will you serve today?

Chapter 16

America's Rise and Fall

Only a short one hundred years ago, Great Britain ruled the world. She controlled or influenced many countries including Ireland, Scotland, India, Australia, New Zealand, Canada, the United States, South Africa and several other nations in Africa. People used to say, "The sun never sets on the British Empire."

At that time, England was known as a Christian nation. She published the King James Version of the Bible and had hundreds of dedicated missionaries all over the world. She had many great religious scholars and leaders like John Wesley and William Booth, who led that nation in prayer and launched a great revival that spread around the world.

Then things began to go wrong. The English people began to turn away from God. In the last several decades, England has fallen on hard times. Less than five percent of her population attends church today. Moral standards have fallen so low they are almost nonexistent. England has lost all of her colonies and her influence is minimal. She is struggling to survive economically. What a sad fate for a once-great nation!

Is America next?

I wonder, is America next? Within my lifetime, I have seen our nation rise to become the most powerful, productive nation on earth. When I was young, churches abounded throughout our towns and cities. We were sending missionaries to every part of the globe to spread the gospel. Our military might was unmatched. We led the world in science, medicine, education, technology, and agriculture.

Our free enterprise system and the dedicated labor of the American worker mass-produced goods at a cost most people could afford. At the same time, our industry provided the jobs and pay needed to improve our standard of living. People prospered. We came to own every conceivable convenience available—cars, appliances, televisions, telephones, and indoor heating, lighting, and plumbing.

We made great advancements in almost every area of life. I have seen transportation advance from the horse and buggy to automobiles and airplanes. Only 60 years ago, Lindberg made his solo flight across the Atlantic. Now men have traveled to the moon, landed, and returned. Today our space shuttles regularly journey into space and back.

Our nation provides one of the highest standards of living in the world. The average American walking through a grocery store will see more food at affordable prices than most people in the world will see in their lifetimes. We enjoy unprecedented wealth and freedom.

But now we, too, are turning away from God. We are forsaking the solid foundation of godly principles this country was built and thrived on. Today we are headed in the same direction that England and other countries have gone. And now we, too, are beginning the slow slide to destruction. What was unthinkable to us only a few short years ago has now become commonplace. We have become too prosperous, too lazy, and too complacent.

We've forsaken our godly principles

First Timothy 6:9,10 describes us well: *People who want to get rich fall into temptation and a trap and into many foolish and harmful desires that plunge men into ruin and destruction. For the love of money is a root of all kinds of evil. Some people, eager for money, have wandered from the faith and pierced themselves with many griefs.*

In my lifetime, I have seen American turn from godly principles like hard work, honesty, integrity, truthfulness, and doing one's best to the worldly principles of getting something for nothing, me first, every man for himself, and anything goes. Our minds and bodies have become lazy. We are no longer productive and we don't care. We have become a nation of paper shufflers, selling foreign products and living off our past prosperity. Our two most common attitudes are "I don't know" and "I don't care."

Everyone seems to have his hand out these days. We've gone from a nation that was proud of its independence and self-sufficiency to a welfare state. No one wants to work hard anymore. The unions say all you have to do is show up for work and you can't be fired. Hard work is laughed at. Mediocrity is the acceptable way.

No wonder our nation is on the decline. Life requires struggle, because by struggling we gain wisdom and strength. When we struggle for something, we value it more. Welfare, on the other hand, breeds

181

weakness and boredom, which lead to alcohol and drug use, crime, and social genocide.

The rich keep getting richer, and the poor and middle classes keep on getting poorer. Today, only five percent of our population holds the majority of the wealth in this country. Yet they are the ones who pay the fewest taxes. Our government is taking money from the workers and giving it to those who haven't earned it and don't deserve it. That kind of continued institutionalized giving discourages personal initiative and self-sufficiency and destroys people's sense of responsibility and self-worth.

The national debt is now measured in trillions of dollars. How much is that? If you had gone into business when Jesus was born and your business was so unprofitable that you lost a million dollars a day every day, it would still take you 700 more years from now to lose a trillion dollars. Our national debt is more than TWICE that amount. At the rate we're going, we will be facing deficits of $15-20 trillion dollars by the year 2000 if we don't do something now.

Our monetary system is ready to collapse. We have built the most gigantic debt in the history of the world, and the only solution our government seems to come up with is to print more worthless money. Our printing presses are turning out more and more money that has nothing to insure its value.

We are now the largest debtor nation in the world, accounting for 60 percent of the world debt. If we don't change our course, within the next few years our economy will be in complete chaos. We will end up like the Germans when their economy collapsed—a wheelbarrow of dollars will not be enough to buy even a loaf of bread.

If America is to survive, we must stop the hand-outs, the grants, the foolish loan guarantees, social welfare, the mediocrity, the something-for-nothing mentality that is destroying us. We must restore our moral foundations, our work ethic, our productivity, and our competitiveness in all areas of life.

Our leaders are to blame

Many of our problems must be laid at the doors of our politicians and government leaders. They have taken the richest economy in the world and bankrupted it in only a few years. Our Congress and Senate are spinning out of control and only a return to biblical principles of leadership can stop their corruption and arrogance from getting worse and worse.

Nearly every day, we hear of some politician who has been indicted for corruption, influence peddling, moral problems, or cover-ups of one kind or another. Our nation's capital has the questionable distinction of being the libido capital of our country, as confirmed by many journalists, political aides, and other observers. Sexual sin seems to be part of the seduction of power. One long-time journalist has stated, "Capitol Hill is the most sexually-charged spot in America."

Every kind of sexual sin is committed by these men and women who are supposed to be our moral and national leaders. For example, Representative Barney Frank (D-Mass.) reported he paid for sex with male prostitute Steven Gobie and had a two-year relationship with him. During that time, Frank paid Gobie thousands of dollars to be his personal aide. Eventually, Gobie was arrested and convicted in Virginia for sodomy, obscenity, and cocaine possession. Frank's punishment? A reprimand from his colleagues.

Most sexual sin on Capitol Hill involves hetero-

183

sexual affairs, which staffers say are as common as fax machines. Representative Donald Lukens (R-Ohio) was convicted for trysting with a 16 year old. Representative Gus Savage (D-Ill.) was accused of fondling a Peace Corps volunteer. Former Maryland Representative Robert Bowman's political career was crushed amid charges that he solicited sex from a 16-year-old boy. Former Washington, D.C. mayor, Marion Barry was convicted of cocaine possession and was a known drug user and adulterer.

And who can forget presidential hopeful Gary Hart's affair with Donna Rice that ended his presidential ambitions? Or the tragic death of a young woman at Chappaquiddick, Massachusetts 20 years ago, when Ted Kennedy's drunk driving turned his car into a watery tomb and cost him his marriage.

Kennedy's ex-staffers report that he continues his immoral living. They say his affairs are too numerous to count. But he has yet to serve even a day in jail and, in fact, serves on the highest judicial committee of the United States, where he helps appoint judges to enforce the laws that govern the citizens of this country.

Do you want this type of people running America and passing the laws you and I have to live under?

Observing our legislators and the "wisdom" of the U.S. Supreme Court, we can rejoice that the court that is truly Supreme does not meet in Washington. Rather, it meets in heaven and is composed of the triune God. No matter what a human Supreme Court says, practices like secular humanism bring the wrath of God upon us.

Our money says, "In God we trust." But the streets are full of pornography, abortions are financed by taxpayers, prayer is outlawed in our schools, and the greed for money influences congressional decisions, corrupting our national morals and destroying this country daily.

Our Senate and Congress are mired in corruption and scandal, as the recent Savings and Loan debacle proved. Nowhere has their self-seeking, money-grubbing attitudes been more apparent than in their handling of the S & L industry in recent years, which led to financial disaster.

In the last five years, one out of every four S & L institutions has closed its doors, and many of those remaining are insolvent or close to it. The Federal Savings and Loan Insurance Company (FSLIC) has also been declared insolvent, and it will take billions of dollars to make the situation right—if that is even possible.

Who is paying for all this mess? Not the politicians who were bribed by S & L officials or who profited handsomely by the S & L mess. No, the bill for the S & L disaster is being paid by the lowly taxpayer, as usual. The people who caused the disaster, and who rightly should be held accountable and punished for it, will escape with their loot and soon be plundering some other American institution.

Gambling is gambling

Many of our state governments have fallen so low that, in order to get money, they are now running some of the largest gambling operations in the world— the lotteries. People are winning—and losing—millions of dollars playing the lotteries. Who operates these "casinos"? Our state governments. A few years ago, the government was fighting organized crime, racketeering, and gambling, and today THEY are the operators! Americans have come to accept it, but gambling is gambling no matter who operates it.

Isn't it time to get rid of these liberal, humanistic politicians who have helped our nation decline to complete immorality? I can't understand why anyone would vote for a liberal candidate who is against everything that God stands for as outlined in His Word. Yet, election after election, these immoral, greedy people are voted back into office. Why? Where are the Christians who ought to be standing up for what is right?

One of the most important things that you, as a Christian, can do is to check out all the candidates for office—city, county, state, or federal—and find out what they stand for. Don't go by what they say but by what they have done. Find out where they stand on the issues of abortion, pornography, profanity, drugs, gambling, God in our schools, etc. If they won't tell you where they stand, don't vote for them.

After an election, write to your leaders and let them know that you want a moral government and that you expect them to do their part. Tell them you aren't going to tolerate any more of the foolishness and immorality that's been going on in government.

Most of all, pray for our leaders. The Apostle Paul wrote, *I urge, then, first of all, that requests, prayers, intercession and thanksgiving be made for everyone—for kings and all those in authority, that we may live peaceful and quiet lives in all godliness and holiness. This is good, and pleases God our Savior, who wants all men to be saved and to come to a knowledge of the truth* (1 Timothy 2:1-4).

Everything began to fall apart
When did the trouble really begin for America? I

believe it began in the 1950s and 1960s, birth years of the Playboy-hedonistic philosophy from which we are still suffering today. Although we didn't realize it at the time, the me-first philosophy of pleasure and greed that began then has had disastrous effects on our nation. We are still reaping its grim harvest, which has affected every area of our society.

During those two decades, everything began to fall apart. Our military suffered two miserable defeats in Korea and Vietnam—even though our leaders didn't have the courage to call them defeats. Americans became disillusioned with the government. Even our one-time allies began losing their respect for us. Countries to whom we had given freely began to hate us, and the cry heard round the world was, "America, go home!"

Our schools, which had once been the best in the world, began to slide. Biblical morality was outlawed and secular humanism was taught in its place. The result has been sexual promiscuity, abortion, drug use, rebellion, and lawlessness among our children. Today, students are graduated from high school who cannot read or write, and thousands drop out.

In the '50s and '60s, our young people began to rebel by the thousands. Our great institutions of learning became hotbeds of anti-government activity, drug use, sex, and all kinds of immorality.

Today, the situation in our colleges and universities continues to decline. Nearly all of this nation's first institutions of higher learning were established for the advancement of Christianity and the glory of God. These include Harvard, Yale, Columbia, Dartmouth, Brown, and Princeton Universities. Their founders all had a strong religious faith. They saw the need for Christian education to help young people accomplish God's will in their lives and become effective leaders in society.

Now you can graduate from any of these schools and never open your Bible or learn any Christian principles. One well-known college, Cornell University on New York's Long Island, was using pornographic films in its sexually-oriented courses and giving students credit for watching pornographic movies, visiting gay bars, and talking with prostitutes.

The decades of the '50s and '60s also saw a great decline in the morality and stability of our government. A President was assassinated. Another President was forced to resign from office because he broke the law. Another indifferently committed adultery with a constant stream of women who paraded in and out of the White House. Other leaders were constantly making headlines because of their ungodly lifestyles.

By their legal rulings, members of our Supreme Court have supported pornography and immorality. They violated our belief in the sanctity of their positions with complete indifference, and their attitude affected us all. The corruption at the very top of our nation filtered down to the majority of America's business leaders, and soon they were being indicted for corruption on an almost daily basis.

The ACLU is destroying us

During the 1950s, an organization came into power that has done much to destroy America. It is the American Civil Liberties Union (ACLU). The ACLU is one of the most harmful organizations in the history of America. It has approximately 250,000 members, nearly 5,000 of which are liberal lawyers, and many governors, congressmen, and senators.

The ACLU is the main force behind the removal

of almost every traditional Judeo-Christian value from our society. Anything that has to do with God is a target for its litigation. The ACLU wants to wipe God completely out of our society, no matter what the moral cost may be to the people. Yet our liberal press continues to present the ACLU as a heroic organization working to protect the individual's rights, instead of the godless, immoral agency that it is.

The ACLU was founded by a communist, Rodger Baldwin, and on its first board of directors were men like Max Eastman, editor of a communist paper, and William Foster, one of the presidents of the American Communist Party. Today, some of its largest contributors are the Playboy Foundation, the Rockefeller Foundation, the Carnegie Foundation, and many other liberal groups.

Baldwin wrote, "I am for socialism, disarmament, and the instrument of violence to destroy all ownership of property and to take control of all freedoms." He also wrote, "Communism is our goal."

In the so-called defense of individual rights, the ACLU has crippled our law enforcement agencies— from the CIA and FBI to local law enforcement agencies—with so many restrictions that they have become almost ineffective in protecting us. The ACLU has won a court action making it illegal to display a simple nativity scene on government property. They have also caused the removal of prayer and God from our public schools and are now working to have "In God we trust" removed from our money.

Bill Murray, son of well-known atheist Madalyn Murray O'Hare, is now a Christian. He has stated that it was the ACLU which helped his mother win her famous case, eliminating school prayers, religious freedom, Bible reading, and the teaching of moral values from our schools. No wonder our schools are becoming centers for assault, sex, drugs, murder, and other crimes.

Today the ACLU is in court fighting to:

+ have the words "under God" removed from our pledge of allegiance,
+ halt all public funding of buses for Catholic schools,
+ prevent the singing of any song about God (such as "Silent Night") at any school or government function,
+ terminate all military and prison chaplains,
+ deny tax-exempt status to all churches and synagogues,
+ prevent any restrictions on the sale of pornography in this country,
+ and, in my opinion, end anything that is moral and American.

How much longer can our nation survive when our children—the future leaders of this country—are growing up in a godless, immoral, anything-goes environment? Why can't we, as Christians, raise up an army of God-fearing activists and lawyers who will fight in our courts to re-establish the basic values and standards this country was founded on? If a group of people can be organized to protect and promote evil, surely a group of concerned citizens can organize a more powerful group which will protect our godly values.

The October 3, 1988 issue of *The Wall Street Journal* carried an article listing several positions endorsed by the ACLU. Among them were:

1. Drugs should not be prohibited by law. The ACLU membership endorses the legalization of every drug from heroin to marijuana. "Gambling, attempted suicide, sexual relations or the introduction of substances into one's own body" should not be crimes (Policy 210).

2. School discipline should be strictly limited. The ACLU has even tried to protect students from searches of their lockers (Policy 76). (This despite the fact that some students bring guns and drugs to school and hide them in their lockers.)

3. Few crimes should be punished by jail time. For those who do go to jail, probation should be authorized by the legislature in every case (Policy 242).

4. Churches and synagogues should lose their tax-exempt status. The ACLU opposes tax benefits for religious bodies (Policy 92).

5. The First Amendment protects all pornography, including child pornography. The ACLU opposes any restraint on the right to create, publish, or distribute materials on the basis of obscenity, pornography, or indecency (Policy 4).

6. Prostitution should be legalized. The ACLU supports the decriminalization of

prostitution and opposes state regulation of prostitutes of both sexes (Policy 211).

7. Homosexuals should be allowed to be foster parents. In 1986, the ACLU radicalized its position on nondiscrimination against homosexuals to include all rights that would qualify gay and lesbian couples for benefits and rights enjoyed by married persons, including the right to become foster parents (Policy 264).

8. Practicing homosexuals should even be allowed to adopt children. In 1991, a Florida judge ruled that a 53-year-old AIDS activist should be allowed to adopt a youngster, stating that "homosexuals have been proven to be capable, loving parents whose sexual orientation is not necessarily adopted by their children."

These and other public positions supported by the ACLU led Pat Buchanan to say, "The ACLU is an organization dedicated to pushing Christianity out of public life."

Does anyone care? I wonder. Former Massachusetts Governor Mike Dukakis said, "I am proud to be associated with this organization [the ACLU]." Here is a man who was proud to be associated with an organization that is trying to eliminate God from our society. Yet, he was the democratic candidate for President in 1988. I don't understand how this could happen!

As our morals decline, so our nation declines

I truly believe that our great spiritual decline of the last 40 years is the reason our prosperity is declining. As our morality falls, so does our wealth and power. The Bible has much to say about God prospering the righteous and diminishing the assets of the unrighteous, and we are seeing that happen today.

The downfall of our nation, which started several decades ago, continues and, today, we are close to losing our country. Ironically, we are losing it to our one-time enemies. The countries we defeated in World War II are now winning the war that really counts.

Japan's goal in World War II was to conquer and dominate the United States. They fought us to win Hawaii and lost. But today they are taking over Hawaii and the rest of the United States to the tune of almost a billion dollars per week.

Not long ago, I spent a Christmas in Hawaii, on the island of Maui. During my visit, I found out, to my amazement, that almost all of the fabulous hotels and resorts on the famous Kapalua Strip are owned by the Japanese.

In addition to Hawaii, the Japanese are gobbling up property along our West Coast at an alarming rate. They now own several ranches of 80,000 acres or more and intend to take over the meat and cattle market of the world. The great American cowboy is now being paid by a new employer—the Japanese.

I wonder if Americans realize that the Japanese now own more property in the U.S. than the whole of their small island nation. When the Japanese tried to take over part of our nation in World War II, we fought them with every ounce of might we had. Today, no one seems to care.

193

The Japanese also have passed us in productivity and technology. For years following the war, the Japanese exported their products into our country and we considered them junk. Today, the quality of their products has surpassed our own. American companies like Philco, RCA, General Electric, and Westinghouse, that once supplied the world with electronics, now have imported foreign-made products into the U.S. and put their labels on them. Most of the products are made in the Far East. Almost all of our car companies are working in partnership with the Japanese, so a truly "American made" car is virtually nonexistent.

Between 1982 and 1990, Japanese direct investments in the U.S. went up over 600 percent. The Japanese now own the majority of our treasury notes, a good deal of our stocks and bonds, and property from coast to coast. They own over 600 manufacturing plants in the U.S., and 30 of their companies could make our Fortune 500 list. Seven of the top 25 banks in the world are Japanese and represent 40 percent of world lending. If the Japanese pulled their money from our banks, they would virtually destroy this nation.

This means we are losing our economic and political independence and, with it, our world leadership. But no one seems to be alarmed. We seem content to be the most entertained people in the world instead of the leaders. As long as our standard of living does not change, we don't really seem to care who owns us.

Not only is Japan buying America, but we are helping her do it. We pay the Japanese over $50 billion a year in our trade balances, as well as spending approximately $40 billion a year defending them with our military. We have defended Japan ever since World War II with our battleships, carriers, war planes, men, and money. Why? The Japanese have been very capable of defending themselves for many years.

The Japanese have totally lost respect for us because we have sold them our birthright so we can continue to live far beyond our means. They are now rewriting their textbooks on World War II to make themselves the victims instead of the instigators of the war. They have lost their guilt, and what they could not accomplish with military might they are now doing with monetary might.

Do our government officials care? Seemingly they don't. They continue to legislate huge handouts to Japan and other countries who have repaid our generosity to them with hate and disrespect. They don't understand that we are in a financial war of survival with countries like Japan and that our nation is at stake. We must win it, or the blood of all the American soldiers lost in World War II will count for nothing!

WE are to blame!

Of course, it would be easy to blame Japan and other countries for our demise, but the truth is, WE are to blame. Our unrighteousness has opened the door to the other nations of the world. Our *immorality* is causing us to decline.

Today we are fighting for our very existence. We need a revival that will turn this nation back to God. As Americans who love our country and would die for it, we must learn to LIVE for it. Freedom is not free. It must be defended, asserted, prayed for, and constantly nourished by a godly way of life. We must restore the biblical foundation our nation once had.

I am writing this because I love God, America, and the citizens of this country. It is still not too late.

We have a forgiving God who will forgive and restore us, if we will get on our knees and ask for His divine help and pardon.

Do you care? Will you help?

Chapter 17

America's Plague of Immorality

In the last 60 years, many of the things Americans have believed and lived by have slowly been stolen away from us. The subtle changes and erosion of our values have crept up on us so slowly we were hardly aware of what was happening.

Solid, basic principles undergirding this nation, based on divine truths and God's laws as set forth in the Bible, and dear to the hearts of our founding fathers, have slowly been crumbling. If someone had described to you, just 20 years ago, the present spiritual and moral condition of America, you might not have believed it. And had the changes happened overnight, there would have been nationwide alarm and concern.

But it all happened so gradually...so quietly. And by the time it was noticed, it seemed that it was too late to do anything about it.

When did we really start to lose America?

When did our God-centered Republic, based on the godly principles of our constitution, become humanistic and atheistic?

When did the Bible become regarded as fiction?

When did lying and cheating become situational ethics?

When did marital fidelity become obsolete, and adultery described as "having an affair?"

When did releasing habitual criminals become justice?

When did saving baby animals become more important than saving baby humans?

When did parenting become the state's responsibility?

When did abomination of homosexuality become simply an "alternate lifestyle?"

When did rest and relaxation become possible only through the use of drugs?

When did the vilest pornography become art...paid for by our tax dollars?

Sin is sin, no matter what you call it. Immorality is evil and deadly, no matter how it is rationalized. God says, *Woe to those who call evil good and good evil, who put darkness for light and light for darkness, who put bitter for sweet and sweet for bitter. Woe to those who are wise in their own eyes and clever in their own sight* (Isaiah 5:20,21).

In the last chapter, I talked about a lot of the problems facing this country, but the greatest problem in the U.S. today is not the ACLU. It's not crooked politicians or our give-me mentality. Our greatest problem is the plague of immorality that is sweeping across our land. It's being manifested as a flood of pornography, profanity, homosexuality, abortion, Satanism, and drug use.

Pornography

The disease of pornography today is almost everywhere you look. It can be found in every neighborhood, on television, in magazines and movies, in our schools and stores. Whether we realize it or not, the pornography peddlers are slowly brainwashing us into accepting immorality and perversion as the natural way of life, and it is affecting our families and our nation.

In Michigan alone, in 1988, there were approximately 20,000 teenage pregnancies, and just under 1,000 pregnancies were girls under the age of 14. Over one million teenage girls get pregnant each year in this country. Three out of five girls in some inner-city schools get pregnant before graduating.

The percentage of men and women who commit adultery is staggering. Divorces are tragic, commonplace symptoms of the breakdown of America's families. Sexual immorality is everywhere. We are in the age of condoms. Our schools now issue them to teenagers. Many state colleges provide condom machines in the boys' and girls' dormitories. Have we completely forgotten about morality?

Even our federal government is in the pornography business. Most people don't know that our government retails pornographic magazines such as *Hustler, Penthouse,* and *Swank* in its thousands of federally-licensed shops on military bases and ships throughout the world. In fact, in some Third-World countries, the United States military has the questionable distinction of being the sole peddler of pornographic material.

It's no surprise that the producers and distributors of this material want us to believe that the U.S. government has a first amendment duty to retail their filthy wares. In fact, the pornographers, the ACLU, and other pro-porn lobbyists are fighting to make the federal government sell obscene material, including the lowest type of child pornography. But these groups are wrong. Like any convenience store or newsstand, the federal government could stop selling this material at any time.

Some of our senators have brought this issue to the attention of the public and our President. As Commander-in-Chief, he can issue an executive order to discontinue the sale of this material, which is clearly degrading and exploitive of women and children. Why not write a letter to the President today and urge him to sign such an order? If the public makes enough of an outcry, he will have to bow to public pressure.

The danger of pornography is that it is addictive. Exposure to pornography, like exposure to narcotics, can be habit-forming and lead individuals to seek increasingly more "hard core" and perverse material. The likelihood of anti-social behavior in a person who reads pornography can grow as this process continues.

Studies by the FBI show that the most common trait of serial killers is their addiction to pornography. Pornography is also heavily read by child molesters, incestuous fathers, rapists, and killers who like to torture and mutilate their victims. The ACLU and the pro-porn lobby would like us to believe that, by protecting pornography, they are simply protecting a form of expression which is victimless. The truth is, people who read pornography are sick and it fuels their sickness and causes many to seek out victims—a child to molest, a woman to rape, an adolescent boy to assault.

Theodore Bundy, a notorious serial killer, was recently executed in Florida. Before his execution, he told Christian family counselor Dr. James Dobson that pornography fueled his (Bundy's) sickness and his urge to rape and kill. He also said that there are many people loose all over America today whose dangerous impulses are being fed each day by violence in the media, especially sexual violence and pornography.

Even so-called "soft core" pornography can have a progressively desensitizing effect. It gradually renders an individual morally numb and personally insensitive to the rights and dignity of others. Look at the number of rapes which take place on our college and university campuses each day. The young men who commit these crimes don't think of themselves as criminals or rapists. They've been brainwashed into thinking their behavior is perfectly normal. They're only giving women what they want, they say. Or they're just doing the things guys do.

Experts say pornography can foster immoral and perverse preoccupations in a user's fantasy life and behavior. It can interfere with his personal moral growth and his development of healthy and mature relationships, especially in marriage and family life. This is the very place where mutual trust, openness, and personal moral integrity in thought and action are so important.

In the worst cases, pornography can act as an inciting or reinforcing agent, a kind of accomplice in the behavior of dangerous sex offenders, child molesters, rapists, and killers.

The spread of pornography

A fundamental reason for the spread of pornography and violence in the media is the pervasive moral permissiveness of our society, which is rooted in the search for personal gratification at any cost. Associated with this is a moral emptiness, which makes personal pleasure the only happiness human beings can attain, and a sense of fatalism. If we're all going to die tomorrow, we might as well enjoy ourselves today.

The Affiliated Broadcasting Company (ABC) is one of the worst—if not THE worst—perpetrators of immorality and violence on television today. In the 1990 Fall season, it had three prime-time shows featuring homosexual characters. "Heatbeat," with its lesbian lovers, was one of its feature programs. In "Hooperman," the main character was a homosexual cop who was constantly being enticed by his female partner to have sex with her.

ABC is using more and more family shows to promote prostitution, drunkenness, and women having babies through illicit sex. And you can hardly find a program on any of the networks these days that doesn't contain a constant stream of profanity. Even seemingly mild-mannered programs like "Mr. Belvedere" contain sexual endorsements.

For example, in one episode of the program, two of the teenage characters are together on a stormy night. The young lady suggests that she sleep with the young man because she is afraid of thunder. The young man responds, "I'm afraid of lightning. Maybe we can merge our fronts!" Such filthy dialogue from teenagers is ABC's idea of good family viewing!

Television executives seem to think that, if they put their filthy programs on after 8:00 p.m. when, supposedly, the children are in bed, everything is okay. But that doesn't make it okay! The kind of filth and perversion that is currently on our airwaves should be totally banned because it is destroying our nation.

One example of this is "Saturday Night Live," on the National Broadcasting Company (NBC). This program constantly promotes immorality and profanity. It makes fun of religion and religious leaders. It puts down our nation and political leaders. And all this in the name of fun!

The Central Broadcasting System (CBS) claims it has a Department of Standards and Practices which is helping it keep the airwaves clean and pure. What a joke! An example of CBS's level of morality took place recently when it took an "offensive" religious program off the air after only one showing.

The perpetrator of this alleged "unacceptable" program was the Catholic Archdiocese of Chicago. CBS had contracted with the church to produce a series of inspirational messages by Cardinal Joseph Bernardin to be telecast once a week in the morning. The first program slipped by the CBS Standards Department but, as soon as it was alerted to this holy "threat," it quickly cancelled the rest of the programs.

The folks in Chicago, just awakening after the previous night's televised diet of murder, robbery, filthy language, deviated sexual behavior, and all the rest, were thus protected by CBS from any godly standards they might have picked up from the Cardinal's program. How sad that our nation has fallen so low that we now accept the filth that comes over the airwaves and in the movie theaters without question, but any mention of God or godly standards is quickly censored.

As I discussed in an earlier chapter, the more filth and perversion we put into our minds, the more filthy and perverse we become. Programming like this on our national networks becomes so commonplace that we don't even think about it. We accept it as the way things are. But that ISN'T the way things are, or not the way things should be!

It's time we did something about the pornography on our airwaves. I think people in general—and

Christians in particular—are fed up with the immorality in our society and will get involved in stopping it. What can we do? We can refuse to watch such filth on television. We can also find out who sponsors these programs and boycott their products until they stop sponsoring them. When a company starts hurting financially, believe me, it will act. The companies and the networks understand and respect the power of money.

There are also several groups around today who monitor television programs and conduct boycotts against the sponsors of bad shows. Get on their mailing lists and get involved. If you think a program is immoral, don't buy the sponsors' products. Write letters to the network and the program's producers.

The movies

Movies today are, in general, even filthier than television programs. They contain more profanity, violence, and blatant sex than television; yet a lot of them ultimately end up on television.

The level of profanity in many of these movies is staggering. For example, characters in the movie, "Midnight Run," used the F-word 125 times in that 122-minute motion picture. That's more than one F-word a minute. Other filthy words were used 45 times for a total of 168 uses of profanity. Since then, the movie has been shown on television, and the TV movie and video guide of 1989 call it "a socko action comedy." Since when did profanity become a laughing matter?

Vulgarity in movies, TV, and videos has progressed beyond anyone's wildest imaginings. It is now beyond the level of any decent or moral person's standards. Many people have quit going to the movies because they are repulsed by the violence, sex, and profanity they see. It seems that writers and producers are incapable of creativity anymore. They think using violence, sex, and profanity in a film will make the proverbial silk purse out of a sow's ear.

A few years ago, for example, no one would have dared make a movie like "The Last Temptation of Christ." The outcry against such a movie would have been unbelievable, and I doubt that many would have gone to see it. In fact, it probably would not have been shown in this country. Yet the film was made and shown, and even some who called themselves Christians defended it.

I believe "The Last Temptation" is the most degrading attack so far on the Person who has done more good for this planet than anyone else, our Lord Jesus Christ. The film is sacrilegious, blasphemous, and anti-Christian. It makes Jesus out to be a man who had sex with Mary Magdalene, who was lustful and indecisive, and who desperately resisted God. It infers that Jesus was unsure about His message and mission. What a lot of Satan-inspired hogwash!

The only reason anyone would dare produce a film like this is because of the complacency of Christians. We should have made our voices heard long ago. It's time we stood up for our Christian rights. Every group in America seems to be protected by the rights movement and the ACLU except Christians. Can you imagine the public outcry that would occur if someone made a movie similar to "The Last Temptation" about the revered civil rights leader, Martin Luther King, Jr.? Even if the movie was completely true and factual, it would be branded as prejudicial, racist, and slanderous.

The debasing of Christian beliefs is not only permitted but promoted by the liberals, the secular humanists, and the ACLU. They shout about their rights and freedom of speech, but they won't let us Christians defend our rights and beliefs.

The broadcasting industry

"If our television programs and movies are so bad," you ask, "then why doesn't the Federal Communications Council (FCC) do something about it?"

I wish I could tell you that the FCC is in court today, prosecuting promoters of filth on the airwaves, but that wouldn't be true. The sad fact is, the FCC is filled with liberal, humanistic individuals who would rather pander to the broadcasting industry to get its support than to stand up for what is right, decent, and moral.

In one year alone, the FCC received over 400,000 complaints, yet prosecuted less than five. In Miami, an announcer regularly solicits young boys for teenage homosexual sex, but the FCC does nothing. In Los Angeles, a radio show explicitly described how "exciting" perverse sex is, but the FCC did nothing. I could cite thousands of lewd and perverse television programs on the air today, but still the FCC does nothing.

The politicians nominate the people for the FCC. So why aren't moral, decent people put on this committee? I can only believe it is because the administration is taking the pro-family vote for granted while passing out political plums to the broadcasting industry. After all, you don't want the media against you when you're running for re-election.

The National Endowment for the Arts

Another perpetrator of pornography is the National Endowment for the Arts (NEA). This federal agency provides taxpayer-funded grants to artists, including musicians, painters, photographers, and performers. Unfortunately, the so-called artists can spend the money they receive from the FCC with little or no accountability for how it is spent.

The 1990 budget for the NEA was $175 million, which came from our tax dollars. How was it spent? Here are some of the "art" projects YOUR money helped fund.

- ✦ One artist who received a $15,000 NEA grant used the money to complete a depiction of Christ on a cross, submerged in urine. He called this so-called work of art, "Pi-Christ."
- ✦ The NEA gave photographer Robert Mapplethrope $30,000 to fund his exhibit of homosexual and perverse photographs. One was a photo of a four-year-old girl with her dress uplifted and her genitals exposed. Another showed a man urinating into another man's mouth. (This is ART?!!)
- ✦ The NEA awarded Mars Artspac $20,000 to fund his photo of Senator Jesse Helms in a large jar of what appears to be urine. Mr. Helms is fighting the funding of this kind of filth by our government.
- ✦ The NEA funded Annie Sprinkle, who performs naked and rubs feces on her body while she shouts profanity. At one of her performances, she bragged, "Usually I get paid a lot of money for this, but tonight it's government funded."

✦ The NEA gave thousands of dollars to sponsor a film festival which featured films for and about homosexual lifestyles, sexual activities, and practices.

Do you want your tax dollars spent to fund this kind of filth? Of course not! Yet when a few congressmen and senators put pressure on the NEA to quit sponsoring these and other "artists," the liberals fought against them tooth and nail. They said anyone opposed to these artists is against freedom of speech and the free expression of art.

Baloney!! I'm not against free speech and I'm certainly not against art. If someone wants to get up on a stage naked, cover herself with feces, and shout obscenities, that's her right. BUT I don't want my tax dollars to pay her to do it. And I don't want my money to go to a homosexual so he can take obscene photos and pass them off as "art."

If the NEA is going to give away your money and my money, we have a right to make the NEA accountable to us for who they give it to. I encourage you to write to your representatives in Washington, D. C., and express your outrage about the kind of pornography the NEA has been supporting. If you don't get involved, you're voting "yes" for the filth and perversion that is destroying our nation.

Drugs

Another part of the plague of immorality sweeping across our nation today is drug use. Pornography and drug use go together, because drugs inhibit a person's morality, while pornography excites his senses. That's why so many murderers, rapists, and child molesters commit their acts while they are on drugs.

In our inner cities, drugs have become the number one cause of death among the inhabitants. Teenagers who grow up on the streets have no moral teachings. Their only creed is to survive. They drop out of school, leave home, and live on the streets. They have no money, no home, no clothes, no food. Someone offers to get them a meal, a place to sleep, and drugs to help them forget their troubles. Before long, the teenagers are hooked, selling their bodies for drugs.

There are millions of people in this country who are in this condition. Some live in nice homes, have good jobs and loving families, but they're hooked just the same. The only things in their future are disease, death, and despair. Does anyone really care? We've become so calloused that most of us just turn our heads and pretend we don't see.

In one 15-block stretch of Manhattan, there are thousands of drifters, hookers, pimps, and drug push-ers. I recently read an account of a ten-year-old boy who was a prostitute. He had toy cars and trucks that his customers had given him.

Thousands of American children are selling themselves to survive. Most are hooked on drugs and sell themselves to pornography users. I absolutely believe that there is a relationship between pornography and these children.

If I were to make an ethnic slur in the press, the ACLU would jump all over me. They would accuse me of hate and of trying to destroy this nation. But they don't worry that pornography and drugs are de-stroying this generation and teaching our young people that they have the right to do what they want, regard-less of who it hurts.

Drug use in this country could be totally wiped out if greed could be eliminated. Money is the fuel that keeps the fire of drug use burning brightly in this country. And we are all to blame. From the President on down to the person in the streets, we close our eyes to what is going on. We aren't committed to winning the war on drugs, and we'll never win it with a half-hearted attitude. We must unite and use everything at our disposal to defeat this enemy.

Instead of each person committing himself or herself to winning the war on drugs, we don't want to get involved. Instead, we give out clean needles, half-heartedly protect our borders, and slap drug users and dealers on the wrist when we catch them. We throw money at the problem, and money isn't the answer.

We are spending over $10 billion a year to fight drugs and billions more dollars on the result of drugs. Yet the March 28, 1990 issue of *USA Today* states that the glut of cocaine in the U.S. is now so great that the drug is within reach of everyone. I repeat—money is not the answer.

The only thing that will win the war on drugs is for this nation to return to the godly principles it was founded on and start practicing moral, caring living. We've got to quit caring about THINGS and start caring about PEOPLE. We've got to give up our materialism and greed and abandon the me-first, pleasure-at-any-cost mentality that is destroying us. Then, and only then, will we see the war on drugs begin to turn in our favor.

Abortion

Another sign of the immorality of our times is the ever-growing number of abortions in our country. Currently, one and a half million babies are aborted

210

every year. That's one out of every four, and the number is growing. In many states, abortion is paid for by the state. Our hearts have become so hardened that we can kill millions of babies a year in their mothers' womb. Why don't we just kill them in their mothers' arms?

The most dangerous place in our world is not in its battlefields but in the wombs of American mothers. Three times every second a baby is born into this world, and one-fourth of those destined to be born in the U.S. will be murdered before birth. Over 24 million babies have died since abortion was legalized in 1974. That's ten times the number of American soldiers who died in all of our wars put together.

Where did the Supreme Court get their authority to legalize abortion? They didn't get it from the Bible or from our Constitution. They didn't get it from the laws of this country or from any previous decision of the Court. The decision was made by a group of secular humanists who bowed to pressure from immoral lawmakers and feminists, and the truth is, they had no real authority to legalize abortion.

Don't believe that just because something is legal it is automatically moral. A Christian has to go by what the Word of God says is moral, not by what a group of humanistic lawmakers say is moral. Murder is murder, no matter what you call it or how many times you make it legal.

A *U.S. News and World Report* article entitled "Abortion: America's New Civil War" quoted a pro-abortionist as saying that the decision regarding abortion should be based solely on what is best for the child. Are any of us wise enough or omniscient enough to know what is best for an unborn child? I think not.

If we could somehow ask an unborn child wheth-

211

er or not he wants to be born, do you think he would say, "Kill me!"? Of course not. There is something within us, as humans, that wants to live, in spite of the circumstances. Life is sacred and we should cherish and protect it.

What can you do?

- ✦ Write your federal and state lawmakers and let them know that you feel abortion is wrong.
- ✦ When election time comes, vote for people who are against abortion.
- ✦ Get involved in a group that works to outlaw abortion.
- ✦ Talk to your friends and family, and educate them about the seriousness and immorality of abortion.
- ✦ Support homes for pregnant mothers and adoption agencies.
- ✦ Work to make positive alternatives to abortion available to every woman and girl who needs them.

You can make a difference, if you care and get involved.

Homosexuality

Another symptom of immorality that is sweeping this country is the rise of homosexuality. In spite of what the liberals try to tell us (and some claim to be Christians), the Bible is very explicit in its condemnation of homosexuality. The Bible says it's wrong, it's an abomination, and God hates it.

Now, I'm not saying God hates homosexuals. He doesn't. God loves them and died for them just like

He did for you and me. God loves homosexuals but He hates homosexuality. Remember the story of Sodom and Gomorrah in Genesis 19? God completely wiped those two cities and their inhabitants off the face of the earth. Why? I read an article once that said God destroyed them because the inhabitants were inhospitable. No, God destroyed them because of homosexuality.

But tragically, homosexuality has become the civil rights movement of the 90s. Although homosexuals represent less than four percent of the nation's population, they wield enormous political clout, far beyond their numbers.

The nation's largest teachers' union, the National Education Association (NEA), has voted in favor of allowing homosexuals to teach all grade levels including kindergarten.

But I believe that when the homosexuals say they want to destroy the family unit, they mean just that. We must not allow a tiny group to deliberately destroy our Judeo-Christian heritage.

The Bible, God's Word, confirms His hatred for the sin of homosexuality. *Do not lie with a man as one lies with a woman; that is detestable* (Leviticus 18:22).

If a man lies with a man as one lies with a woman, both of them have done what is detestable. They must be put to death; their blood will be on their own heads (Leviticus 20:13).

Today, homosexuality is on the rise. Not only is it becoming more widespread but it is also becoming more acceptable. As I mentioned earlier, prime-time television shows now have homosexuals and lesbians as their main characters.

There is currently a bill before Congress, known

213

as HR-709, which has been labeled a "Gay Bill of Rights." It would:

1. Legalize homosexuality and lesbianism.
2. Criminally prosecute all churches, schools, businesses, and local, state, and federal agencies which refuse to hire homosexuals for any reason.
3. Criminally prosecute any individual—you or me—who refuses housing accommodations to homosexual/lesbian couples.
4. Set a precedent by which the homosexual/lesbian subculture can legally:
   a. repeal all sodomy laws and laws governing the age of consent, so as to lower the age for children to legally participate in perverted sex acts;
   b. allow the legal marriage of homosexual/lesbian couples and their adoption of children;
   c. require all public schools to create sex education courses taught by homosexuals to show that their lifestyle is a moral, healthy, and normal alternative to heterosexuality.

The shocking truth is, many homosexual/lesbian groups have already accomplished many of these moral outrages through state and local legislation. The Congressional "Gay Bill of Rights" would simply enforce it nationally. Is this what you want? Will our children be safe if this bill is passed?

Some religious organizations have gone the way of the world and ordained homosexuals and lesbians as ministers. Notice I said "religious," not Christian organizations. Any organization that truly believes and practices the Word of God will never knowingly ordain a homosexual any more than it would ordain a drunk, an adulterer, murderer, etc.

We now spend more on AIDS than on any other ailment—more than on cancer and heart disease combined. There is no question that AIDS springs from the practice of homosexuality.

How much longer can we tolerate this kind of immorality and ungodliness? It is no wonder that Satanism is on the rise throughout the country. Crimes involving Satanism have become so numerous that cities and towns across the nation are training their police officers in how to detect and deal with Satanism.

It's time we stood up and let our voices be heard. Every believer is called upon to be a good soldier for Christ. In these days, especially, we must pray that we will be strong and vigilant in the battle between good and evil. We must act now to stop the tidal wave of immorality that is sweeping across this nation and destroying it.

America's fateful choice

It seems to me that we, as Americans, have to make a fateful choice of what we want for our nation, for ourselves, and for those who will come after us (if there is an "after"). As I see it, there are three options:

1. A religious society dominated by the church, or the totalitarian rule of kings or a government based on the concept of "divine right."
2. A secular humanist society dominated by the theory that there is no God—that people can achieve anything these choose in their own power.

215

3. Liberty and justice for all, respecting the beliefs and rights of Christians, other religions, and atheists alike.

A governmental system built around the first option is why the first settlers left England and came to America.

The second option pretty well describes our country today.

The third option is what our founding fathers envisioned and tried to establish this nation upon. Most of them had a deep faith in God, but rather than force their beliefs on others, they established a nation which provided liberty and freedom *for* (not *from*) all types of religious expression.

Today, the concept of "separation of church and state" is being used by the Congress and the Supreme Court as a means to eliminate all mention or recognition of God from our learning institutions—indeed, from all of society. This was NOT the intent of our founding fathers, who sought to establish the United States on the moral and spiritual foundation of the Bible.

In fact, the work of the constitutional convention was done amid much prayer and in the righteous fear of God. No less a person than Thomas Jefferson expressed his concern over the morality and behavior of his countrymen by saying—

"In deed I tremble for my country when I reflect that God is just, and that His justice cannot sleep forever."

Why would a just God allow such evil?

On occasion, I've heard people pessimistically assert that they find it difficult to believe in a God who would allow the sickness, poverty, and evil which exists in the world today—even in America. If God is a good and loving, all-powerful being, why doesn't He stop such suffering and misery?

I once heard a story about two men walking through a slum area which speaks to this concern. One of the men was a Christian, the other a barber who claimed to be an atheist. As they walked through the crumbling neighborhood, the barber pointed out the street people in their poverty, eating out of garbage cans, the filth and disease, the evidence of crime, drug abuse, alcoholism, etc. "I can't believe in a God of love who would let these conditions exist," he declared.

A half-block further along, the men saw a street dweller huddled against a building. He had long, stringy, dirty hair, and two weeks' growth of stubble on his face. The Christian man turned to the barber and said, "Surely you can't be a very concerned or responsible barber. How could you let people like this live around here without a haircut or a shave?"

Very indignantly, the barber replied, "I can't help it if he chooses to live like that! He's never come to my shop and given me a chance to fix him up."

"Then don't blame God for allowing sinners to continue in their evil ways," said the Christian. "He gave His life to provide salvation for all who will call on His name. He stands at the door of each person's heart, knocking, seeking to come in. If they refuse His love and pardon, it's not His fault."

The Word of God is very clear and emphatic about the choice before us. *This day I call heaven and earth as witnesses against you that I have set before*

217

you life and death, blessings and curses. Now choose life, so that you and your children may live (Deuteronomy 30:19).

I implore you to make the right choice today. Choose God. Choose life. Do it now. You might never get a second chance.

God help us, and our nation, to make the right choice today.

Chapter 18

America's Last Chance

America today is almost dead. Our government is in chaos. Our morality is minimal at best. Our economy is teetering on the edge of destruction. We're losing—or have already lost—all the things that once made this nation great. We're infected with the virus of sin and we're dying.

What can we, as Christians, do? Is there hope for this country? I believe there is! I was pronounced dead. Then I was given electric shocks and brought back to life. If America is shocked severely enough, maybe she, too, will come back to life. If people would only see how low we have fallen and turn from their sin, I believe God would restore our nation and make us the great nation we once were.

We can make a difference

Evil is taking over so many people's lives. Satan knows his time is short, so he is going forth with great power to destroy this country. But we must realize that God is still on the throne, and we can still have a time of great revival. The Bible says, *The one* [Jesus] *who is in you is greater than the one who is in the world* (1 John 4:4). If Christians would take a stand for Christ and what is right, we could turn this nation back to God.

Our world is filled with people whose hearts are failing them for fear of the things that are coming upon the earth (see Luke 21:26). There are wars and rumors of war, famine, and disease. We are surrounded by drugs, pornography, greed, ungodliness, political corruption, injustice, and selfishness. People have lost their hope for the future and have plunged themselves into pleasure seeking and self-worship.

But, in spite of the wickedness and hopelessness around us, we can make a difference for Christ in our world. What can we do?

First, we must give our number one priority to evangelism. We must confront the world with the gospel of Jesus Christ, without apology, just as Peter did at Pentecost. The more evil the world becomes, the more desperate the need to spread the gospel. Jesus' mandate for Christians is still the same: *Go and make disciples of all nations, baptizing them in the name of the Father and of the Son and of the Holy Spirit, and teaching them to obey everything I have commanded you* (Matthew 28:19,20).

The greatest thing that can happen to a person is for him or her to become a child of God. The second greatest thing is to reach out to someone else and tell them how your experience of salvation can also be theirs.

How many leaders, pastors, and Christians let month after month, year after year go by without being used of the Holy Spirit to lead even one person to Christ? Are they good and faithful servants or have they forgotten their greatest priority in life?

The main priority of any church should be evangelism—reaching the lost and bringing people to a true understanding of salvation that leads to a spiritual rebirth. If this is not happening, a church becomes a self-righteous, sanctified, selfish social club. Jesus taught us through the years that His ministry and top priority was evangelism, and it should be ours, too. All of us must have the desire to reach the people around us who are facing a Christless eternity.

Second, we must train believers to have a "Christian world view." This means we recognize that our whole existence was built upon the God of the Bible instead of upon sinful man. Right and wrong are determined by God as written in His Word.

The secular world says any kind of art, movie, or magazine is permissible, no matter how debasing, because someone wants it. The Christian says it's wrong to debase man with pornography and immoral art. The secular world says the end justifies the means in business and politics. The Christian insists on honesty and integrity and knows that all powers and authorities are to be subject to God.

The secular world implies that the family has outgrown its usefulness and can now be dispensed with. Christians reject this idea and assert that the family is a divine institution, not to be tampered with. The secular world says man is only a material being and his existence ends at death. Christians assert that man does not live by bread alone and death is only the beginning of eternity.

In short, we need a new race of people, with a different view of the world, who are willing to fight and die for their cause. God is calling us to rise to the occasion as we never have before. *Have nothing to do with the fruitless deeds of darkness,* Ephesians 5:11 tells us, *but rather expose them.*

For example, Ted Turner owns and operates three powerful TV cable networks which influence millions of Americans. He claims that anyone who believes in Christ is a fool. By personal example and media influence, he promotes free sex, drinking, and a disregard for Christian ethics.

Working on the theory that people can only get out of their minds what is put into them, Mr. Turner is gradually filtering filth into the programs on his networks. After a time, even once-decent Americans will accept the video fare they see as normal until anything will be acceptable. Within five years, merchants of godlessness and filth, like Mr. Turner, can control the minds and hearts of Americans nationwide.

Children in school don't learn a subject in a few days, but they gradually absorb the theories over an extended period of time. They think, react, and then accept the things being taught.

Will we allow the world and Mr. Turner to "teach" us and control our minds—or will we turn back to the Bible and the teachings of God?

Third, we must quit supporting the immorality makers. That means we must quit patronizing carnal, immoral movies. We must stop watching immoral home videos and television programs. And we must stop buying filthy books and magazines. If there was no market, there would be no product. This kind of filth is destroying our minds and morality. We can boycott companies that produce and sponsor this kind of trash. We can write letters to these companies and let them know that we're tired of the filth and anti-Christian garbage they're trying to feed us.

We must stop being the invisible majority

Fourth, we must be heard through the media—

television, newspapers, and magazines. We must let the media know that we are not going to be the invisible majority anymore, that we want fair, unbiased representation in the media. We must demand that the media give us the truth instead of constantly presenting the liberal, secular humanists as heroes and Christians as villains.

Fifth, we must join together to fight the groups which are trying to eliminate God from our nation and take away our Christian rights. Everyone else is screaming for their rights, and it's time we stood up for our rights as Christians. We must fight the liberal, humanistic groups like the ACLU that are working to destroy us. The ACLU brings its lawsuits against everything that is moral and biblical in this nation. But if every Christian would take a stand and all join forces, we could defeat the ACLU and all the liberals.

Support national Christian groups

There are two Christian groups forming to fight the ACLU bunch. The Rutherford Institute is making a real difference in restoring our vital freedoms. This nationwide team of aggressive attorneys and concerned citizens is dedicated to defending the constitutional rights of religious people. It operates through a rapidly growing state-by-state network of chapters and provides legal service without charge to hundreds of people each year nationwide.

The Institute has targeted five priority areas:

1. To preserve free speech in public areas, including public schools.
2. To protect the right of churches, church schools, home schools, and other religious

organizations to operate freely without improper state intrusion.

3. To defend parent rights and family autonomy.

4. To support the sanctity of all human life.

5. To assist individuals in totalitarian countries, oppressed for their beliefs.

Rutherford student chapters and summer internships provide special training and experience for law school students seeking to use their legal skills in the defense of religious freedom. The Institute provides services without charge and relies on tax-deductible contributions from individuals for support. If you would like to know more about the Institute, you can write its national headquarters at: The Rutherford Institute, P. O. Box 7482, Charlottesville, VA 22906-7482.

A second group that has started recruiting lawyers to form a team to challenge left-wing groups like the ACLU is the AFA. Don Wildmon, the executive director, is establishing a network of lawyers who will work with the AFA in their respective areas across the country. AFA will furnish the training and resources for their lawyers to help in the cases they handle.

In addition to the first amendment rights of Christians, AFA's legal team will also be involved in the enforcement of obscenity laws. They will be a very valuable asset in our court battle for Christians and Christian families.

For more information write: AFA, P.O. Drawer 2440, Tupelo, MS 38803.

We are already winning some victories

These two groups can and will make a difference

in our battle for morality. Already there have been some changes and victories in the battle for Christian rights.

We can complain and express concern about the future, but a more effective way to help turn America around for God is to support organizations like these, who are fighting for our rights in court and in the law-making process. If you are really concerned, send contributions and talk to your lawyer friends about donating part of their time to help re-establish God's laws in our courts. The ACLU has an army of more than 2,000 lawyers and several volunteers who are eager to turn America into a secular humanistic society with no morals, and to remove God completely from America. Are we as committed?

Just five years ago, Bridget Mergens, a 17-year-old high school student, was a new Christian and wanted fellowship with other Christian kids. She asked her school principal for permission to start a Bible club at school. He denied her request. At that time, her school allowed more than 30 student clubs to meet on campus after school hours.

Bridget presented a copy of the Equal Access Act to her principal, but he told her it didn't apply to the school. Then Bridget addressed the local school board. The board voted down her request, 6 to 0 with one abstention.

With the help of an attorney from the National Legal Foundation, Bridget then took her case to the U.S. District Court. She lost again, but Bridget persisted. Eventually, her case went all the way to the Supreme Court, where she won.

Justice Sandra Day O'Conner wrote the majority opinion for the Court, affirming the Equal Access Act. She said the Court makes a crucial distinction between "private religious speech," which is constitutionally protected and "Government religious speech," which is prohibited. This distinction permits student-led Bible clubs to meet on school grounds and also protects a child's right to carry a Bible to school or to pray on his own.

It is the responsibility of Christians to take advantage of this ruling and the Equal Access law. Our children have the opportunity to provide a support system to other kids in an environment that is often hostile to Christian values.

If you would like more information about the Equal Access Act, write for your free booklet, entitled "A Guide to the Equal Access Act." Write to: Christian Legal Society, 4208 Evergreen Lane, Suite 222, Annandale, VA 22003.

Sixth, we must let our politicians know that we're fed up with the status quo and we want things to get better. We must put in office decent, moral people who keep their word and work for the good of the country. We must stop re-electing individuals who make anti-Christian laws and live ungodly lives.

We must check out every office seeker and find out what his or her standards are. Then we must vote for the one who lives a godly life and has the qualifications we are looking for. Also, we must continually communicate with our elected officials on issues we believe in. We cannot be the silent, invisible majority anymore.

Seventh, we must put God back in our education. How can we teach our children morality if we do not give them the true basis for that morality—God? We must teach them the value of hard work, personal integrity, self-sacrifice, team work, and self-reliance.

We desperately need Christians to speak out and

help form moral character and the work ethic in our young people. We need people who care with their whole hearts, who dream big dreams, and who work as hard as they can to inspire our children and give them confidence and hope for the future.

You must know Christ personally

Eighth, (and most important), we must each have a personal, genuine, relationship with Jesus Christ that includes daily prayer and Bible study. Too many church members have sold out their desire for God to comfort and acceptance. They want to be part of the "liberal movement," which includes some of the most ruthless, immoral people in our country.

The New Age Movement is making an enormous impact on the hearts and minds of millions of Americans. The movement, in short, is a composite of beliefs from Eastern religions involving reincarnation, pantheism (everything is God), psychic powers, and even aspects of witchcraft. New Age leaders teach that "I am God...you are God...each one of us has the same potential to be God." Interestingly enough, this was Satan's first fatal claim and the lie he used on Adam and Eve. Now, through the New Age Movement, he's trying to impose it upon everyone else.

This damnable lie is embraced by secular humanists, Eastern religions, Satan worshipers, and various occultic groups, headed by deceived people like Shirley MacLaine, who claim to have enough power in themselves to become gods. But when their turn comes to die, their bodies will return to dust and their spirits will forever be separated from the true God who created us and the world we live in.

What did all these false gods create? How many have come back from the grave as Christ did?

Today, many profess to believe in reincarnation and claim to have lived previously as another person. They say that, at death, they will come back again. Has anyone ever proved reincarnation by demonstrating a comeback? Houdini, perhaps the greatest illusionist of all time, claimed he would return. But he hasn't come back. Yet multitudes continue to accept these philosophies which lead to eternal separation from God.

The Bible says, *For the time will come when men will not put up with sound doctrine. Instead, to suit their own desires, they will gather around them a great number of teachers to say what their itching ears want to hear. They will turn their ears away from the truth and turn aside to myths* (2 Timothy 4:3,4).

If Christians are content and do nothing to stop these evil forces—America will die!

So many churches today have replaced spirituality with religiosity. The average church gives you a lot of sweet nothings instead of the Bread of Life. They have become mere social clubs where you go to meet your friends and have a good time. They're not places where you hear about a holy God, judgment, heaven, or hell.

We must study our Bibles and know what God has said. Homosexuality is wrong. Murder is wrong. Stealing is wrong. It doesn't matter if the Supreme Court says these things are okay, the Bible still says they're wrong and those who practice them will be punished by God.

Why are so many Christians reluctant to move into a deeper relationship with Christ? Because the way to grow in Christ is the way of the cross: the way of self-denial and unconstitutional surrender of one's own will to God's will. This is the way Christ calls all of us. *"If anyone would come after me, he must deny himself and take up his cross daily and follow me. For whoever wants to save his life will lose it, but whoever loses his life for me will save it"* (Luke 9:23,24).

Choose you this day

God is giving you and me a choice today—whether we will live for Him or not. It's the same choice He is giving our nation, and our future depends on what we choose. It's the same choice He gave the Children of Israel in Deuteronomy 30:15-20:

See, I set before you today life and prosperity, death and destruction. For I command you today to love the Lord your God, to walk in his ways, and to keep his commands, decrees and laws; then you will live and increase, and the Lord your God will bless you in the land you are entering to posses.

But if your heart turns away and you are not obedient, and if you are drawn away to bow down to other gods and worship them, I declare to you this day that you will certainly be destroyed. You will not live long in the land you are crossing the Jordan to enter and possess.

This day I call heaven and earth as witnesses against you that I have set before you life and death, blessings and curses. Now choose life, so that you and your children may live and that you may love the Lord your God, listen to his voice, and hold fast to him.

What will your choice be? Will you choose eternal life with God and life for our nation? I pray so! Every person who has ever lived has had to face this decision. History records that some made the right decision—God's life—and some made the wrong decision—death and destruction. I want to share some of their stories with you.

James A. Garfield

James A. Garfield grew up in poverty and had little formal schooling. He worked as a farmer, carpenter, and boat hand. At the age of 20, he wrote one of the clearest descriptions of salvation I have ever read:

"Today I was buried with Christ in baptism and arose to walk in newness of life. For as many as have been baptized into Christ have put on Christ."

Garfield became a minister and served in various churches. Later, he attended William College, graduating with honors in 1856. Garfield was convinced that it was a Christian's duty to participate in public affairs. He won a Republican seat in the Senate in 1859 and distinguished himself by denouncing slavery and secession.

When the Civil War broke out, Garfield became a lieutenant colonel. He later resigned his commission to enter the U.S. House of Representatives. He led in establishing the U.S. Department of Education and later became House Minority Leader. In 1880, Garfield was elected to the U.S. Senate and was then nominated for President.

He was the only preacher to be elected President. On July 2, 1881, less than four months after his inauguration, Garfield was seriously wounded by a deranged man. He died on September 19, 1881. He had served Christ throughout his life and was ready when death came. He had made his world a better place.

Lew Wallace

Lew Wallace was a famous general and writer. In the first part of his life, he was an avowed atheist. For two years, Wallace studied in the leading libraries of Europe and America, gathering information to write a book that would forever destroy Christianity. While writing the second chapter of his book, Wallace suddenly found himself on his knees, crying out to Jesus, "My Lord and my God."

Because of the solid, irrefutable evidence he found, Wallace could no longer deny that Jesus was the Son of God. Later, Wallace wrote *Ben Hur,* one of the greatest novels ever written about the time of Christ.

C. S. Lewis

Similarly, C. S. Lewis, a professor at Oxford University in England, was an agnostic who denied the deity of Christ for many years. But he, too, submitted to Jesus as his God and Savior after studying the overwhelming evidence of His deity. He wrote many books that have helped change many lives. His book, *Mere Christianity,* has helped thousands—including my friend Chuck Colson—find Jesus Christ.

Charles Colson

Charles "Chuck" Colson was the chief counsel to President Richard Nixon. His whole life centered on politics. A former Marine, Chuck once bragged that he would walk over anybody who got in his way. When the Watergate scandal broke, Chuck got caught in the middle of it and was sent to jail.

A friend witnessed to him and, after reading Lewis'

book, *Mere Christianity,* Chuck gave his life to Christ and was completely changed. He is now a new man, with his priorities centered on Jesus Christ. Chuck realized that the only Answer for depraved man is Jesus. Jail, prison terms, punishment—none of these things can truly change a person's heart. Only Jesus can perform that miracle.

Chuck is now chairman of Prison Fellowship ministry and directs several thousand workers in taking the good news of Jesus Christ throughout the world. He says he would not trade his job for that of the President because he has the most rewarding job there is—leading people to God.

John Newton

John Newton was seven years old when his mother died. She was a devout Christian who read the Bible and prayed daily. God had given John many talents—writing, singing, oratory, poetry, etc. When he was 11, he went to sea. At age 18, he became captain of a ship and got involved in the slave trade.

Newton thought nothing of throwing overboard any slave he disliked. He wrote poetry and songs blaspheming God. He had many black mistresses and was a frequent visitor to the brothels of his day.

Newton's fellow sailors said his very presence on board a ship brought a curse on them. They talked many times about throwing him overboard.

One day Newton's ship was in a great storm. The ship filled with water, and the sailors were certain they were going to die if they didn't do something. They thought Newton was the cause of the storm, so they threw him overboard. Two sailors at the back of the ship realized this was mutiny and knew they would be hanged when they returned to England. They quickly threw a harpoon at John, which caught him in the leg, and they hauled him back aboard.

Newton went to his cabin to think. He knew he had been given a second chance at life. He picked up a Bible and it fell open at Galatians 1:23,24. He read, *"The man who formerly persecuted us is now preaching the faith he once tried to destroy."* John knew the verse was talking about the Apostle Paul, but its description also fit him. From that day on, John felt that God might be preparing him for the ministry.

When he arrived back in England, he began meeting with other Christians and soon became their leader. He started a church and it grew, and his reputation spread all over England. He was called to the pastorate of the Church of England at Olney. The congregation was small in the beginning, but with John's evangelistic fervor, many of the nobles attended his weekly meetings to hear the converted sea captain tell of God's amazing grace and power.

During his Olney ministry, Newton wrote many hymns. Among them were, "How Sweet the Name of Jesus," "There is a Fountain Filled With blood," and perhaps his most famous and beloved hymn, "Amazing Grace." This song tells how God's grace saved one of the most vile sinners and changed him into a great man of God.

AMAZING GRACE
Amazing grace, how sweet the sound,
That saved a wretch like me!
I once was lost, but now am found;
Was blind, but now I see.

'Twas grace that taught my heart to fear,
And grace my fears relieved;

How precious did that grace appear
The hour I first believed!

Through many dangers, toils and snares,
I have already come;
'Tis grace hath bro't me save thus far,
And grace will lead me home.

When we've been there ten thousand years,
Bright shining as the sun,
We've no less days to sing God's praise
Than when we first begun.

Newton worked very hard to end the slave trade
in England. Finally in 1833, England passed a law,
freeing her slaves and condemning the slave trade.
When Newton died, he had this testimony inscribed
on his tombstone:

> *John Newton, clerk,*
> *once an infidel and Libertine,*
> *a servant of slavers in Africa,*
> *was by the rich mercy*
> *of our Lord and Savior*
> *Jesus Christ,*
> *preserved, restored, pardoned,*
> *and appointed to preach*
> *the Faith*
> *he had long labored*
> *to destroy.*

When John was 80, a friend suggested he quit
preaching. "What!" he shouted. "Should this old
slave ship captain, who hated God for so long, stop

preaching while he can still speak? NEVER!" Newton made a decision to serve God.

William Murray

When he was a teenager, William "Bill" Murray
was very active with his mother, Madalyn Murray
O'Hare, in atheistic causes. Bill was the plaintiff in
the court case to end prayer in public schools, which
led to the Supreme Court ruling that took God and the
Bible out of public schools.

Bill says his mother was not only an atheist but
also a Marxist, which teaches that self is the center of
the universe. She tried to immigrate to the Soviet
Union but was rejected. She continued her fight against
prayer in classrooms until June 17, 1963, when the
Supreme Court ruled that prayer and Bible study were
unconstitutional in public schools.

In 1977, Bill felt increasing concern that he was
supporting atheism. As he studied it and talked to
atheist friends, he saw that atheism was anything but
positive. Two years later, he began to think about his
life. He concluded that there had to be a God because
there certainly was a devil. Bill knew he had walked,
talked, and obeyed the devil's commands for years,
and the devil had destroyed Bill's life, marriage, family, and health. Bill was an alcoholic and was fast
becoming the personification of evil.

Bill began attending Alcoholics Anonymous,
where he learned that the only way to win in his
struggle against alcohol was through his reliance upon
God. Bill read the Book of Luke in the Bible and
discovered that Jesus Christ was the only Answer to
all of his problems. He gave his life to God.

Since his conversion, Bill realizes that removing
prayer and the Bible from our schools is the main

cause of the destruction that is running rampant through these institutions today. Bill has written several books about his testimony and has appeared on many television shows.

Like Newton, Bill hated God and preached against Him for years. Yet God, in His mercy, touched his life and made him a new man. Bill had a choice and he chose Jesus.

There are many other examples of great men who chose God:

Charles G. Finney was a lawyer who turned to evangelism and turned millions to Christ.

Dwight L. Moody was a shoe salesman who preached to tens of millions. Moody built a college in Chicago, preached in England and throughout America, and was visited by President Lincoln.

Billy Sunday turned from baseball to evangelism and was on fire for Christ. He led millions to God.

There have been many who did not choose God

History also records many who made decisions against God. Voltaire, the great French intellectual and atheist, was panicked at the prospect of death. He offered his physician half of his fortune if he would give him six more weeks of life. For all his genius, Voltaire didn't know he could have all eternity in a place far better than any place he had ever known, just for the asking.

Voltaire said Christianity would be gone in 30 years' time, but today the house he lived in is home to a publishing company that prints the Bible.

Over 50 years ago, a group of men gathered for a meeting in Chicago. In attendance were ten of the world's most financially successful people, including the presidents of the world's largest steel company, utility company, and gas company, the greatest "bear" in the commodity market, the president of the New York Stock Exchange, the president of one of the world's largest banks, a member of the President's cabinet, head of one of the world's largest monopolies, the greatest wheat commodity dealer on Wall Street, and the most successful speculator on Wall Street.

You would think that this group of the world's most successful men would have learned the secret to life, but this was not the case. While they had found the secret of making money, they did not know the secret of peace and joy.

Twenty-five years later, the president of the largest steel company in the world, Charles Swabb, died in bankruptcy.

Samuel Ensel, president of the world's largest utility company, died as a fugitive in a foreign country, penniless.

The president of the world's largest gas company, Howard Hopson, was insane.

The country's greatest wheat commodity dealer, Arthur Cotton, went insane and died overseas, insolvent.

Richard Whitney, one-time president of the New York Stock Exchange, served several years in prison and was finally released.

Albert Fall, a former member of President Harding's cabinet, was convicted of a crime and sent to prison. He was finally pardoned so he could die at home.

The greatest "bear" on Wall Street, Jesse Livermore, committed suicide.

Ivan Kruger, head of the International Match

Corporation, one of the world's greatest monopolies, committed suicide or was murdered. The truth was never established.

The president of the world's largest bank, Leon Frazer, committed suicide.

The man who was known as the "Boy Wonder" of Wall Street committed suicide.

All of these men learned the art of making a living very well, but not one of them learned how to live. They made their choices but, unfortunately, they did not choose wisely.

Ralph Barton, one of the great cartoonists of this nation, pinned this note to his pillow before he took his life—"I have gone from many friends, great successes. I have gone from wife to wife and from house to house, visited many countries. But I am fed up with inventing devises to keep me going from day to day."

There was once a man whose only desire in life was to have money. So he worked night and day until he had accumulated over a billion dollar's worth of assets. He wanted fame, so he went to Hollywood and became a film maker. He wanted sexual pleasure, so he paid many beautiful women to indulge in sex with him. He wanted power, so he made secret deals with two of our nations' presidents until he had them in his control.

This man did everything he knew to do in order to have a full, rich, fulfilling life. But all his riches, experiences, and possessions did not bring him joy and happiness. Although he was the richest man in the world, he ended his life emaciated, afraid, and sick. He had a sunken chest, long fingernails, black teeth, tumors, and innumerable needle marks from his drug addiction.

The man's name was Howard Hughes. He thought his life consisted of what he owned, but all his riches did not buy his way into the kingdom of God. Jesus said, *"Do not store up for yourselves treasures on earth, where moth and rust destroy, and where thieves break in and steal. But store up for yourselves treasures in heaven, where moth and rust do not destroy, and where thieves do not break in and steal. For where your treasure is, there your heart will be also"* (Matthew 6:19-21).

Howard Hughes had a choice. Sadly, he made the wrong one.

Revival can come

God said, *"If my people, who are called by my name, will humble themselves and pray and seek my face and turn from their wicked ways, then will I hear from heaven and will forgive their sin and will heal their land"* (2 Chronicles 7:14).

This can only happen when the Methodists, Catholics, Presbyterians, Baptists, and Pentecostals—all Christians—unite in prayer and put Christ first in their lives. Then, and only then, will we have revival in America.

Patrick Henry said:

"I wish I could leave you my most cherished possession—my faith in Jesus Christ. For with Him you have everything. Without Him, you have nothing at all."

Napoleon Bonaparte stated,

"I know men and I tell you that Jesus Christ was no mere man. Between Him

and every other person in the world, there is no possible term of comparison. Alexander the Great, Caesar, and I have founded empires. But on what did we rest the creations of our genius? Upon force. Jesus Christ founded His empire upon love, and at this hour millions of men would die for Him."

We, as Christians, must break the barrier if we truly want a revival. Millions of people live in unimaginable conditions. When we cannot break the barrier of sin and take the good news of Jesus Christ to those who need Him most, we are all losers. The Church keeps preaching to the same members every Sunday, and the lost die and go to hell without hope.

If America doesn't have a meaningful revival that brings millions into God's kingdom, including the moral liberals and the secular humanists, we, as a nation, will continue on the road to destruction. But if we truly and deeply repent, it would change America.

President Calvin Coolidge said:

"America was born in a revival of religion and will die if neglected."

America is ripe for revival. So many people are seeing their lives, families, and loved ones destroyed. They are looking for Someone who will give them help, joy, peace, and the promise of eternal life.

What will you choose? Will you choose to be a part of the problem or a part of the answer? It's up to you. I'm so thankful that God gave me a second chance at life and the opportunity to share my story with you. I urge you today: make Jesus Christ your number one priority in life. Give Him everything you have and are. Live for Him and invite everyone you can to do the same. Let revival in America begin with you!

APPENDIX

Top Sponsors of Sex, Violence, Profanity - Fall 1990

| | Sexual Content | | | | | | | |
| | Sex Outside Marriage | | Sex Inside Marriage | | Skin Scenes | Total | Profanity | Violence |
	Intercourse	Comments	Intercourse	Comments				
NBC	51	200	9	15	28	303	428	329
ABC	24	78	3	6	35	146	321	197
CBS	42	126	4	18	65	255	464	226
Total	117	404	16	39	128	704	1213	752

American Family Association encourages contacting the leading sponsors and/or their local dealers to voice concern. AFA also encourages individuals to boycott the leading sponsors of sex, violence, and profanity.

Rank	Company	Score
1	American Honda Comp.	20.14
2	S. C. Johnson & Sons Inc.	19.40
3	Duracell USA	18.36
4	U. S. Sprint	17.64
5	Sony Corp. of America	16.75
6	Anheuser-Busch	16.32
7	Pfizer, Incorporated	15.82
8	Nissan Motors	14.42
9	H. J. Heinz Company	14.36

Score based on the number of sex, violence, and profanity incidents sponsored with each 30-second commercial ad run. Based on monitoring done by American Family Association during the Fall network sweeps period, October 28-November 24.

ADDRESSES:

1. **American Honda Company,** Pres. Yoshihide Munekuni, 100 West Alondra, Gardena, CA 90248, Phone 213-327-8280. PRODUCTS: Honda motor vehicles.

2. **S. C. Johnson & Sons, Inc.,** Chrm. Samuel C. Johnson, 1525 Howe Street, Racine, WI 53403, Phone 414-631-2000, **TOLL FREE: 1-800-558-5252.** PRODUCTS: Agree shampoo, Aveeno bath products, Bravo wax, Brite floor wax, Carnu polish, Clean & Clear wax, Curel skin lotion, Duster Plus cleaner, Edge shaving cream, Enhance perfume, Favor polish, Fiberall laxative, Fumigator, Future floor coating, Glade room odorizer, Glo Coat floor coating, Glory rug cleaner, Halsa shampoo and conditioner, J-Wax, Johnson Wax, Klear floor coating, L'envie perfume, Off insect repellent, Pledge wax, Pride wax, Raid insecticide, Rain Barrel fabric softener, Shout stain remover, Skintastic moisturizing body gel, Soft Sense lotion, Step Saver cleaner.

3. **Duracell USA,** Chrm. C. Robert Kidder, Berkshire Industrial Park, Bethel, CT 06801, Phone 203-796-4000, **TOLL FREE: 1-800-346-9470.** PRODUCTS: Durabeam flashlight, Duracell batteries and flashlights, Mallory batteries.

4. **United Telecommunications, Inc.,** Chrm. Paul H. Henson, P.O. Box 11315, Kansas City, MO 64112, Phone 913-676-3301, **TOLL FREE 1-800-877-4646.** PRODUCTS: U. S. Sprint phone service.

5. **Sony Corporation of America,** Chrm. Masaaki Morita, 9 West 57th Street, New York, NY 10019, Phone 212-930-1000. PRODUCTS: CBS Records, Columbia Records, Columbia Pictures Industries, Lowes theaters, Sony electronic products.

6. **Anheuser-Busch Companies,** Chrm. August A. Busch III, One Busch Place, St. Louis, MO 63118,

Phone 314-577-2000, **TOLL FREE 1-800-325-1488**, PRODUCTS: Break Cake snack cakes, Budweiser beer, Busch beer, Busch Gardens, Colonial bread, Eagle beer, Eagle Brand roasted nuts, Earth Grains muffin batter, El Charrito Light entrees, Hawaiian Kettle potato chips, Hot 'N Fresh breads, King Cobra malt liquor, Master Cellars wines, Merico dough breads, Michelob beer, Natural Light beer, Sea World parks.

7. Pfizer, Inc. Chrm. E. T. Pratt, Jr., 235 E. 42nd Street, New York, NY 10017, Phone 212-573-2323, **TOLL FREE 1-800-527-3606.** PRODUCTS: Airspun Powder Essence mousse, Barbasol shaving cream, Ben-Gay rub, Chateau fragrance, Coty perfumes, Desitin skin products, Emeraude perfume, Equalactin laxative, Exclamation perfume, Hai Karate cologne, Iron cologne, Lady Stetson women's cologne, Nuance perfume, Plax mouthwash, Shape'n Shadow eye kit, Sophia perfume, Stetson cologne, TZ-3 athlete's foot ointment, Unisom, Visine eye drops.

8. Nissan North America, Pres. Tom Mignanelli, Box 191, Gardena, CA 90247, Phone 213-532-3111, **TOLL FREE: 1-800-NISSAN-1,** PRODUCTS: Infiniti automobiles, Nissan motor vehicles.

9. H. J. Heinz Company, Chrm. Anthony J. F. O'Reilly, Post Office Box 57, Pittsburgh, PA 15230, Phone 412-456-5700. PRODUCTS: Alba sugar-free hot cocoa mix, Amore cat foot, Candle Lite Dinners, Crispy Crowns potatoes, Crispy Whips potatoes, Heinz food products, Mrs. Goodcookie cookies, Nine Lives cat food, Ore-Ida potato products, Skippy dog food, StarKist canned tuna, Steak-Um, Superman hot cocoa mix, Weight Watchers foods & classes.

American Family Association
Post Office Drawer 2440
Tupelo, MS 38803